BRAVING SORROW
TOGETHER

THE TRANSFORMATIVE POWER
OF FAITH AND COMMUNITY
WHEN LIFE IS HARD

ASHLEIGH SLATER

MOODY PUBLISHERS
CHICAGO

Unless otherwise indicated, all Scripture quotations are from The Holy Bible, English Standard Version® (ESV®), copyright © 2001 by Crossway, a publishing ministry of Good News Publishers. Used by permission. All rights reserved.

Scripture quotations marked NLT are taken from the Holy Bible, New Living Translation, copyright © 1996, 2004, 2007 2013, 2015 by permission of Tyndale House Foundation. Used by permission of Tyndale House Publishers, Inc., Carol Stream, Illinois 60188. All rights reserved.

Scripture quotations marked KJV are taken from the King James Version.

Scripture quotations marked MSG are from The Message, copyright © 1993, 1994, 1995, 1996, 2000, 2001, 2002 by Eugene H. Peterson. Used by permission of NavPress. All rights reserved. Represented by Tyndale House Publishers, Inc.

Scripture quotations marked NIV are taken from the Holy Bible, New International Version®, NIV®. Copyright © 1973, 1978, 1984, 2011 by Biblica, Inc.™ Used by permission of Zondervan. All rights reserved worldwide. www.zondervan.com. The "NIV" and "New International Version" are trademarks registered in the United States Patent and Trademark Office by Biblica, Inc.™

Scripture quotations marked TLB are taken from The Living Bible copyright © 1971. Used by permission of Tyndale House Publishers, Inc., Carol Stream, Illinois 60188. All rights reserved.

Edited by Linda Joy Neufeld
Author photo: Ted Slater
Cover and interior design: Erik M. Peterson
Cover photo of painted stones copyright © 2016 by CACTUS Blai Baules / Stocksy (966794). All rights reserved.

Library of Congress Cataloging-in-Publication Data

Names: Slater, Ashleigh Kittle, author.
Title: Braving sorrow together : the transformative power of faith and
   community when life is hard / Ashleigh Slater.
Description: Chicago : Moody Publishers, [2017] | Includes bibliographical
   references.
Identifiers: LCCN 2017025909 (print) | LCCN 2017036206 (ebook) | ISBN
   9780802496256 | ISBN 9780802416599
Subjects: LCSH: Loss (Psychology)--Religious aspects--Christianity. |
   Grief--Religious aspects--Christianity. | Communities--Religious
   aspects--Christianity. | Fellowship--Religious aspects--Christianity.
Classification: LCC BV4905.3 (ebook) | LCC BV4905.3 .S58 2017 (print) | DDC
   248.8/6--dc23
LC record available at https://lccn.loc.gov/2017025909

ISBN: 978-0-8024-1659-9

We hope you enjoy this book from Moody Publishers. Our goal is to provide high-quality, thought-provoking books and products that connect truth to your real needs and challenges. For more information on other books and products written and produced from a biblical perspective, go to www.moodypublishers.com or write to:

Moody Publishers
820 N. LaSalle Boulevard
Chicago, IL 60610

1 3 5 7 9 10 8 6 4 2

Printed in the United States of America

Praise for *Braving Sorrow Together*

Reading *Braving Sorrow Together* is like sitting across from the best kind of friend—a friend who has been down the well-worn path of suffering and can listen, empathize, and offer gentle guidance for the journey ahead. If you are walking through your own "weeping years," Ashleigh's book will free you to grieve your loss while clinging to the hope that you are never alone in your grief.

KELLY GIVENS
Editor of *iBelieve.com*

Braving Sorrow Together is a healing salve for the hurting heart. Ashleigh's words offer comfort and hope as they lead you to both trust in and to lean on the Lord for His strength.

DARLENE SCHACHT
Time-Warp Wife Ministries

Braving Sorrow Together is a powerful and practical ministry tool for the community of Christ, especially when its members need comfort and care. This book not only shows us what to do when we don't know what to say, it encourages us to fight the urge to run from the pain and suffering of others. Instead, we are empowered to forge strong relationships during the not-so-nice times of life, reflecting the gospel as we do. Highly recommended!

KAREN EHMAN
Proverbs 31 Ministries speaker and *New York Times* bestselling author of *Keep It Shut* and *Listen, Love, Repeat*

Ashleigh hasn't given us a textbook or psychological treatise on grief—she's given us an armchair, a tissue, and a listening ear. With each story of loss, she turns us back to the grace of the gospel. Watching her grapple with her own sorrows gives me the courage to explore my own.

LISA ANDERSON
Director of Boundless.org and author of *The Dating Manifesto*

Grief and loss are real. They're hard and even harder to talk about. But in her beautiful, honest new book *Braving Sorrow Together*, Ashleigh Slater fearlessly wrestles with the hard questions, the nitty-gritty issues of grief, loss, and mourning. Filled with real-life stories, practical actions, and sound advice, anyone mired in the trenches of loss will find godly direction and wise counsel as they read this book. Ashleigh has walked the path and knows it well. Let her experience guide you and give you hope.

KATE BATTISTELLI
Author of *Growing Great Kids: Partner with God to Cultivate His Purpose in Your Child's Life*
Mother of GRAMMY award winning artist Francesca Battistelli

If you are struggling with grief or anxiety, you are not alone. In this book, you will find a kind and honest travel companion in Ashleigh Slater.

ARLENE PELLICANE
Speaker and author of *Calm, Cool, and Connected: 5 Digital Habits for a More Balanced Life*

Asheigh Slater provides personally vulnerable insights in addressing an important, heartfelt need—the issue of suffering. She examines a wide range of difficult life situations, including relationships, health, work, etc. and shows how faith and community are keys to navigating this season. *Braving Sorrow Together* provides biblical wisdom, practical application, and true stories that will help you grow through pain and sorrow and embrace God's best for your life.

Susan G. Mathis
Coauthor, *Countdown for Couples* and *The ReMarriage Adventure*

Loss is a dark and painful reality of life in a fallen world. Ashleigh reminds us in *Braving Sorrow Together* that we don't grieve our losses alone. We need to brave our sorrows together with our church community, reminding each other that "loss is not a forever part of your story."

Christina Fox
Author of *A Heart Set Free* and *Closer Than a Sister*

Ashleigh's ability to communicate the importance of braving sorrow while reminding us of God's love is a breath of fresh air. I have no doubt the words on these pages will encourage many who feel alone in their grief.

Carlie Kercheval
Cofounder of Learning to Speak Life Books™

As I read *Braving Sorrow Together*, it truly felt like I was sitting across from Ashleigh sharing moments of togetherness in a conversational way. In a culture where slowing down and acknowledging grief is nearly unacceptable, Ashleigh pulls back the curtain, allowing us to be vulnerable enough to acknowledge the pain of loss. She writes not as a spectator of loss but as a participant, sharing the truth that helped her and practical ways that the reader can come alongside someone who has suffered loss of any kind.

Sarah Bragg
Host of the *Surviving Sarah* podcast

Braving Sorrow Together is an incredibly helpful and compassionate book for anyone who is hurting or suffered loss. And isn't that the case for most all of us? So many people go through life experiencing grief, disappointment, and heartache. Yet in spite of this camaraderie of sadness, we feel more alone than ever. Ashleigh Slater brings both hope and practical help to a topic that so many of us feel, but hardly know where to turn. Her book is one that you'll want to read for yourself, as well as give to a hurting friend.

Lisa Jacobson
Club31Women.com

To Olivia, Ava, Savannah & Dorothy,
may you always trust the Author of your stories.

CONTENTS

FOREWORD

"I am so sorry."

Once again I lay on the cold ultrasound table staring through tear-filled eyes at the doctor. She had no explanation. The steady and hopeful beating of my unborn child's heart stopped at twenty weeks.

"I just doesn't understand why," she said. "I am so sorry." Just like that, I was thrown back into territory that was all too familiar—for the fifth time.

I had become terrified to hear the words, "I am so sorry." And rightfully so. There is a groaning and an aching that comes not from labor pains, *but from losing a child*. I have felt the pain of the labor of four children, who I cherish, but I have also felt the pain of losing five more, who I have not yet met.

None of us know when grief will envelop us or when the hard times will come, but inevitably they do. It is a part of life. Painful as these times are, the grieving gives birth to growth in us. God uses these times to mold us into the man or woman of character He wants us to be.

It has been over seven years since my last miscarriage and life has dealt many other blows since then. But I can look back and say with confidence that God has used my experiences to shape me into who He wants me to be. I know that in God's economy, no tear is wasted; no pain is unseen; no heartache goes unnoticed; no agony is unobserved.

Perhaps you are reading this today and you are in the midst of your own heartache. It might be new and scary and heartbreaking or it might be from years ago. On many occasions the psalmist's words have been mine, "Thy word is a lamp unto my feet, and a light unto my path" (Ps. 119:105 KJV).

When the psalmist penned these words, he likely had a picture in his mind of something we would only understand if we traveled back to that time.

Several thousand years ago an ancient oil lamp, so small it barely covered one palm, was used to light the way when you were traveling in the dark. Like an ancient flashlight, it had a small opening at the very end where only a small flicker of light could escape. I can only imagine that they would have to hold it extremely close to the ground, having just enough light to even make out where their next step would be.

The psalmist is reminding us that when we follow Christ, we never truly are walking in the dark. It might feel like it. Everything around us might lead us to believe we're wandering, wounded sometimes, into the abyss. But God's Word, His precious and powerful promises, are piercing the darkness and illuminating our path, shedding light on His character, promises, and plans.

No matter what you have experienced, even if you can barely see, He has a path lit for you. In *Braving Sorrow Together*, Ashleigh Slater extends an invitation for us to keep walking, lean into the heart work He is doing in us, keep being faithful to Him, and let our community of believers love and support us through it all. As we walk with God, we never truly walk in the dark.

Looking beyond the pain, we can walk with Jesus through afflictions and into the arms of the Father, all the while trusting that the person we are now is not the same person we will be at the end of our journey.

Thank God.

RUTH SCHWENK
Founder of TheBetterMom.com
Coauthor of *Pressing Pause* and *For Better or For Kids*

PROLOGUE

"I will not say, do not weep, for not all tears are evil."
— J. R. R. Tolkien[1]

Have you ever been cautioned about a movie *before* you watched it, only to view it anyway?

I have.

It was several years ago, when my oldest daughter, Olivia, was in the fifth grade. I offhandedly mentioned to one of my sisters, "We're planning to watch *The Bridge to Terabithia* as a family this weekend."

Turns out, she'd seen the film.

"It's sad," she advised me. Her words offered not in a nostalgic "you just have to watch it" sort of way, but in an admonitory "are you positive you want to do that to your kids" kind of tone.

Sad? I thought. *My four girls can handle sad. Not a problem.* After all, this wouldn't be their first "sad" movie. I was confident, verging on cocky, that they could handle a film about kids and a magical wood and whatever tragedy it presented.

Twenty minutes after the movie ended, I discovered I was utterly and completely wrong, at least with regard to one of my children. I should have taken my sister's caution more seriously, perhaps even read a review full of spoilers so as a parent I'd know what to expect.

If you've never seen the 2007 film (and, yes, this is your official spoiler alert), it's the tale of two fifth-grade friends, Jess and Leslie. Together, the two create an imaginary kingdom in the woods named Terabithia where they escape the difficult realities of life. That is, until one day, when Leslie suddenly and unexpectedly dies in a tragic accident while Jess is on an outing with their music teacher. It's an outing that he chose *not* to invite Leslie to join.

While my three younger daughters seemed unfazed by this on-screen tragedy, Leslie's death hit Olivia . . . like it did Jess . . . hard. As I sat down on the end of her bed to tuck her in that night, I noticed her eyes were red.

"Are you okay?" I asked.

She bravely fought to hold herself together, but her efforts failed. Tears, along with the words, "It was just so sad," burst forth.

Right before me, my ten-year-old daughter broke.

Suddenly, it struck me that this fictional character of Leslie fit too closely into Olivia's day-to-day reality. Like my girl, Leslie was a creative and imaginative blonde-haired, blue-eyed fifth grader. And, because of this, Olivia—more so than her sisters—identified with this full-of-life little girl who was no more.

As I watched my daughter start to cry, I broke too.

I knew the sorrow she felt wasn't something I could fix for her. There was no kissing of boo-boos or Band-Aids that would restore the little bit of innocence now gone, that could cure this heightened awareness that the world wasn't as safe or as fair as she'd believed two hours earlier. She understood now, at a deeper and more mature level than our miscarriage five years earlier had taught her, that death could claim kids, too. This was a reality worthy of mourning.

We sat there and I offered Olivia the only thing I had to give her: my tears and my empathy. It was true I couldn't fix the sting of loss, but I could be there for her as she felt it. I could pray with her that the God who writes my story and hers would bring her comfort.

And with this book, I hope to do the same for you.

I love what N. D. Wilson writes. He says, "Life is a story. All of it. From left to right."[2] When it comes to this story of life, my experience has taught me that loss is a devastating and unavoidable part of it. Loss often serves as a jarring reminder to me that I'm not the author of my life's book. God is.

Back in January 2010, my husband, Ted, and I had no idea that we'd one day look back and remember that month as the beginning of what I call our "weeping years." It was a two-year period marked by miscarriage, multiple job losses, feelings of betrayal, panic attacks, antidepressants, cross-country moves, and even suicidal thoughts. The intensity of these years changed the way I look at and interact with grief.

It's not that my life had been absent of bereavement before 2010. I'd suffered my share of loss in my twenties (you'll hear some of those stories throughout this book) and even prior to adulthood. Growing up, there were out-of-state moves every three to five years, a mom who almost died from a placental abruption when I was twelve, a sister born two months premature, and the 1993 "Storm of the Century" that flooded our home with nine-foot waves as we watched from a second-story balcony. But as hard as these childhood challenges were, as well as the ones that were scattered throughout my twenties, there was something about going through an intense, prolonged season of grief as a thirtysomething adult and a mom myself, that changed me in ways I didn't anticipate or expect.

This book is birthed from the changes that took place in me during those weeping years. Within these pages, you'll find a collection of stories and reflections on loss and how it's okay—good even—to allow ourselves and others time to gradually and fully grieve.

Yet, I hope that's not all you find.

I pray that as you read, you'll also be gently and lovingly reminded that the Author of my story, and yours, is present amid our loss and grief.

Now I understand firsthand that when you're in the deep, dark trenches of pain and sorrow, it's frustrating to have others offer statements such as, "God is good and you can trust Him," or "God works *everything* out for good." When life is hard and loss is fresh, that's often not helpful. Instead, it can feel hurtful and dismissive.

In the days following my miscarriage, a well-meaning friend told me the story of someone she knew who'd lost a preborn baby ten years earlier. She shared all that God had done in this woman's life during that decade and told me I should be encouraged. Her words stung. I felt painfully silenced by her "God will work this out" comments and pushed to move forward before I was even close to ready. What I really needed was permission to grieve in my own way and in my own time. I wanted others to affirm, as I did for Olivia, that my current reality was worthy of mourning.

Throughout this book, I will continually assert that your loss *is* deserving of grief. There will be times, though, where I'll also share how I strive in my own sorrow to trust that even when life gets hard, God stays good. Even when I feel like He's far away, He's near. And, in those moments, I may encourage you to believe the same. I may remind you that this Master Storyteller is carefully crafting each of our individual tales and in His active, caring presence there is hope as we encounter loss. Please know that, when I do, it won't ever be flippantly or lightly.

This is also a book about community and about having, as Shauna Niequist writes, a home team. She describes this team as those "middle-of-the-night, no-matter-what-people."[3] I don't believe you and I are destined to be lone heroes, withstanding the heartbreaking plot twists on our own. Instead, God wants us to depend on Him and to, as Olivia and I did that evening, brave sorrow together. He wants us to be raw and vulnerable and broken with each other.

As you read, I hope that you'll feel less alone in your grief. That, as you see yourself and your loss in my loss and the loss of others, you might experience what my husband, Ted, calls a "camaraderie of sorrow," or what Scripture refers to as a "fellowship" of suffering (Phil. 3:10 KJV). May the stories and reflections in this book encourage you to actively seek comfort in the Author of our faith and the "me too" of community.

CHAPTER 1

CONTROL

*"We can make our plans, but the Lᴏʀᴅ
determines our steps."*
— **Proverbs 16:9** (ɴʟᴛ)

I bet you didn't know I'm afraid of the dark," a five-year-old Savannah informed me, her manner so matter of fact.

I wanted to whisper back, "Me too," but I stopped myself. This third-born daughter of mine was too young and too dependent on me to bear the burden of my solidarity.

What I left unspoken was that sometimes my dread of the dark was debilitating. There were times, too many to number, when the mere suggestion of venturing out after the sun set triggered a panic attack. I'd even spent a couple of years turning down girls' night invitations if they required I be out after dusk.

For as long as I remember, I've struggled with fear at some level.

For as long as I remember, I've struggled with fear at some level, but I haven't always been severely afraid of the dark. It's an apprehension that surfaced after the miscarriage as I suddenly found myself suffering postpartum, grief-triggered anxiety attacks and irrational fear. The attacks happened in situations where I felt a loss of control, places—such as the dark—where I couldn't clearly assess my surroundings to determine whether I and those I loved were safe from harm.

The recent death of our preborn baby through miscarriage had acutely reminded me, more than any other loss I'd personally experienced, that control was not mine. Safety wasn't guaranteed. And beyond that and even more terrifying to me, it highlighted in broad strokes of ugly neon yellow, that God—who *was* in control—had allowed one of my kids to die.

My first panic attack hit nineteen days after our obstetrician informed us there was no heartbeat. One minute, I was fine. The next, my heart began to race, my breath grew scarce, and I flashed back to the ultrasound room. It took at least ten minutes for my body to return to a semi-calm state.

The first attack led to a second, and a third. Before long, I experienced multiple attacks a day as my irrational fears increased. I was even unable to walk into a dark room in my own house without dread.

In a matter of weeks, I went from being a happily pregnant mom to someone who struggled to function physically, emotionally, and mentally. Not only had I been helpless to control whether my preborn baby lived or died, I now failed to govern how my body reacted to the grief.

My obstetrician recommended I take antidepressants. After careful consideration, I filled the prescription, and continued to for the next two and a half years. While the medication didn't erase the anxiety or fear, it lessened the intensity and frequency of both. It kept me balanced and functional as we spent the next two years navigating job loss, financial pressures, and multiple moves.

After we relocated to Atlanta from Colorado Springs, via short stints in both Chicago and Missouri, I determined to try life without the medication. I was deeply grateful for its stabilizing influence on my body, but I was also curious to see if I could now function without it. It had been a couple of years since the miscarriage, Ted had a steady job, and we'd settled into what seemed to be a restful season.

I said "goodbye" to the meds, and quickly realized I was saying "hello again" to more frequent panic attacks. They consistently came in those moments when I felt the most out of control. There were the busy playgrounds where I couldn't quickly and easily headcount my kids, or the multiple times our credit-card number was stolen.

With the increase of panic attacks, I also found myself struggling more intensely again with the dark. There were evenings when I pushed myself to bravely go out and meet a friend. Yet there were also days, weeks even, when I vulnerably shared that I couldn't leave my house after the sun set because my anxiety was too great.

It was at this point that Savannah confided in me her fear of the dark, and it was at this juncture that I understood I needed to come to terms with living an out-of-control life.

THE OUT-OF-CONTROL LIFE

A loss of control isn't confined to those of us who suffer miscarriages or anxiety attacks. Every bereavement we'll talk about in this book serves as a keen reminder that you and I aren't ultimately in command of our lives.

Sure, we carry the power to make decisions that direct and impact how our days, months, and years are spent. We conclude what profession we'd like to pursue, which college to attend, whom and when we want to marry, how many children to have, and whether we drink coffee from Starbucks or brew it at home. Yet, aside from where we indulge our caffeine cravings, our decision to accomplish a goal doesn't guarantee that everything goes as planned.

We can't force a particular college to accept us, and once we do earn a degree in a chosen field, that doesn't ensure we successfully work in it. Marriage may not happen on our ideal time line or to the individual we initially hope; and sometimes, even if it does, we might not celebrate a tenth or twentieth or fiftieth wedding anniversary. And, when it comes to kids, sheer will doesn't promise pregnancy, a bureaucratic red-tape-free adoption, or that those we nurture outlive us.

My friend Denise McDowell understands well what it's like to slowly and painfully realize we aren't in control of our lives, and to surrender to the One who is.

....

"The LORD had closed her womb" (1 Samuel 1:5).

Six words that struck fear in my heart and sealed a coffin of grief in my head. It did not say Satan, the environment, the doctors, the misspent youth, the waiting too long, the disbelief, the not eating the right foods, or breathing the wrong air. It said, "The LORD had closed her womb." Argument over, door closed, cigarette out.

There is no arguing when what you hear, and Scripture confirms, is that your God, whom you have turned to for strength, hope, kindness, and most of all, goodness, deliberately does this to one of His children. In giant red letters, it's confirmed. He is in control, and you are not. He determines who will give birth, who will be born, and who will not.

Every one of those realities came crashing down on me in the spring of 1999, after our one and only failed in vitro fertilization (IVF) attempt after five years of trying to conceive. The Lord and I had been on exemplary terms before that season. I believed in Him. He believed in me. We walked hand-in-hand in the garden of youthful faith, and then, He disappeared. He abandoned our agreement.

Before, I did what was right, and He rewarded. Now suddenly, I did what was right, and He punished. He closed my womb for no apparent reason. He left my side to go and bless everyone else with children, even ones who didn't do everything right.

When we used to walk together in the garden of faith, I got to control lots of outcomes. I wanted to be the first in my family to graduate from college, and He made it happen. I wanted to fall in love with a combo Robin Williams/Cary Grant/Bono man of God. He made it happen. I wanted to be happy. He made it happen. It was the perfect relationship. He asked. I obeyed. I asked. He obeyed. It was the thing of Christian fairy tales.

Then a word more putrid than "putrid" entered my life. Infertility was foreign and excruciating. It meant hundreds of doctor's visits, a thousand inconclusive tests, and what felt like millions of dollars. All of these produced the same results: barrenness, nothingness, loss, and grief.

I prayed, searched, read, studied, exercised, stood upside down, all in an attempt to right the wrong that was taking place. Where had He gone? Where had my secret formula gone? Where had my control gone? It all evaporated.

My husband was in seminary, and I worked full-time for a church. Time and funds were extraordinarily limited, but we were surrounded by a loving community of people who offered their support. We were gifted with the means to make one last try to create a family through the costly procedure of IVF, and we went for it. It was our last attempt at controlling our own destiny. It was an abysmal failure, and the tantrums and mournful weeks that followed matched any you'd witness at the grocery store checkout line with a toddler.

All the faith, obedience, study, patience, long-suffering, etc., we put into our god-sized slot machine produced nothing but more heartache.

All the faith, obedience, study, patience, long-suffering, etc., we put into our god-sized slot machine produced nothing but more heartache. We never hit the jackpot in our futile waiting and striving for our dream family.

On one of the more intense tantrum days, my husband held me as I stayed a puddle on the floor trying to understand what else I could do to possibly change the outcome of our situation.

He lovingly said the words that crushed and infuriated me.

"Baby, God is in control."

And as if someone poured gasoline on my fire of fury, I quipped back, "I KNOW HE'S IN CONTROL! That's the problem! I need to know HE'S GOOD!"

I finally surrendered my seat of control. I cried "uncle" along with a myriad of other pleas. Like Hannah who looked drunk to Eli in 1 Samuel, I was inebriated with my own tears of loss. I controlled nothing. The Lord controlled everything. The surrender was nearly more than my soul could bear.

While I wish I could say that I rose up out of those ashes like a phoenix and soared through the next few months confident of His love and grace, it's not true. I crawled daily to Him. I begged daily for relief. I laid bare all I knew of myself to all I knew of Him, and I buried my invisible biological children. Their coffin was made of hopes and future plans, and their gravesite was the nursery I walked past every day. With them, I buried my sense of control forever.

For months I floated along, carried by nothing more than a scriptural promise that "your grief will turn to joy" [NIV]. My heart couldn't bear another loss, another affront to my surrender, so I did nothing but exist. I pursued nothing, sought out no solution, unturned no remedy or formula. I watched hope disappear.

And without warning or even real invitation, the Lord grabbed my hand and said, "Let's walk again, shall we?"

I didn't know if I wanted to hold His hand again. He was quite controlling, and quite unkind. Why would He want to be with me now? What more did He want?

"Are you willing to let Me write the story now and always?" was all I was asked by my Sovereign.

"Yes," knowing now that my response could be an invitation for more pain and grief.

"Then walk with Me all the way to China. I have two children waiting for you. They've felt nothing but loss as well. You will be perfect for each other."

I'd love to say that from that day forward He only blessed and never closed another place I thought would be forever open. There were quite a few caskets to follow, but this time I had a tight grip on His hand. I let go only of my illusion of control.

....

Maybe you can relate to Denise. Perhaps you too have questioned God's goodness as you've painfully faced infertility. Or, like me, you struggle with anxiety and panic attacks. It's possible that your loss of control is related to another area of life such as marriage, a job, your health, or the heartbreaking trauma of past abuse.

Whatever your individual story may be, I don't have any easy answers for you. The truth is, there aren't any. Both my story and Denise's clearly remind us of that. What I can offer you, though, is biblical encouragement that has sustained and gently challenged me in my own grief. One of the places I've discovered this help is in the story of Jesus, a storm, and twelve fearful men.

JESUS, A STORM, AND TWELVE FEARFUL MEN

Both the gospels of Matthew and Mark include an account of Jesus and His disciples crossing the sea in a boat. Prior to boarding, Matthew tells us that Jesus spent the day healing the sick, which included Peter's mother-in-law (Matt. 7:14–16). Mark notes that Jesus also taught both the crowds and His disciples using parables, or simple stories with spiritual lessons.

Between the healing and the teaching, there's no doubt Jesus was physically exhausted by the time He and His friends' voyage began. Because of this, He decides to use the commute as an opportunity to take a nap. Mark tells us, "He was in the stern, asleep on the cushion" (Mark 4:38).

As Jesus sleeps, a storm arises. The wind becomes so powerful that it creates huge waves. These waves furiously break against the boat and begin to fill it with water. If you've ever experienced hurricane-like conditions, as I have, you understand how terrifying this is. Strong currents of water driven by massive gales of wind aren't conditions any of us want to be in when we're on a boat.

His friends panic. All signs point to their vessel sinking, and them drowning. Even the fishermen among them, who are skilled boaters and have likely experienced their share of storms, realize they aren't in control of this one. They can't calm the wind or the waves. They can't even troubleshoot their way out of this one with their sailing expertise.

Frantically, they wake Jesus up. Matthew tells us they exclaim, "Save us, Lord; we are perishing" (Matt. 8:25), while Mark records their words as, "Teacher, do you not care that we are perishing?" (Mark 4:38). Either way, it's clear these grown men are dismayed that their friend and teacher sleeps at such a time as this.

At the disciples' prompting, Jesus gets up and responds to them, as well as to the storm. Jesus' reactions here offer me two teachable moments to ponder as I navigate situations where I, like the disciples, grieve a loss of control. Perhaps they're moments you can glean something from too.

Attitude is everything

Jesus' response to His disciples is "Why are you so afraid? Have you still no faith?" (Mark 4:40 NLT). I've often wondered why Jesus doesn't reply to His friends' panic with reassuring words such as, "It's going to be okay. I've got this. Don't be afraid." After all, this was a scary, life-threatening situation. He could've cut them some slack and shown greater compassion. Yet, the more I dig into this story, the more I believe that Jesus' response directly relates to His disciples' attitude.

These twelve men didn't forget that Jesus was in the boat with them. They didn't question His presence in their lives or in the midst of the storm. They knew He was there and they understood that He had the power to intervene in some manner. It was this knowledge that they allowed to negatively contribute to their demeanor when they woke Him.

Think back to how Mark notes they responded. He quotes them as saying, "Teacher, do you not care that we are perishing?" (Mark 4:38). From this, it appears that Jesus' friends were agitated by His seeming lack of interest in their circumstances. His state of sleep communicated to them an absence of concern for their safety and an ignorance of the severity of the situation. We see from their use of the word "perishing"—which both Matthew and Mark include—that they wanted Jesus to feel as alarmed as they did. We aren't told the tone they employed when waking Jesus, but I wouldn't be surprised if it contained hints of irritation and accusation. It's possible that if Jesus' friends had woken Him up with a different attitude and perhaps a different phrasing, His response may have been, "It's going to be okay. I've got this. Don't be afraid." But they didn't.

They appear to have forgotten all that they've witnessed of His character.

The storm also seems to have facilitated short-term memory loss in the disciples, which may have further fueled their approach. While these men did remember that Jesus was in the boat with them, they appear to have forgotten the day's earlier events: the healing of the sick, the casting out of demons, the parable after parable about the importance of faith. When the opportunity arises for them to exercise trust in Jesus' ability to be there for them in stressful situations, they instead question whether He even cares at all. They appear to have forgotten all that they've witnessed of His character.

Like the disciples in the boat that day, I often find myself in situations I have no control over. It's frightening to realize that there isn't anything I can do to fix my circumstances, and it's frustrating when my skills and expertise afford me nothing. As a result, I sometimes do what the disciples did here. I don't forget that God is present in my life when hard things happen, but I'm inclined to question whether He actively cares. It can feel like God the Father, whom Scripture tells us doesn't "slumber" (Ps. 121:3), is napping and lacks interest in helping me. As Denise needed to know, I too ponder, "God, are You good to me?"

In these instances, I'm faced with a decision. Will I question God's care for me with irritation and accusation, as the disciples seemingly did, or will I hold firmly to my belief that God is lovingly attentive to me even when I feel like He isn't?

As I've battled panic attacks, this choice has loomed before me constantly. Yes, the years have taught me that there are practical actions I can employ to lessen the frequency and intensity of the anxiety. But the years have always shown me that no matter what I do, whether on medication or not, panic attacks are a part of my current story. Regardless of how much I pray, exercise, or actively identify triggers, I still have them regularly.

This biblical story reminds me that I have the power to respond differently than the disciples when faced with my own "storms." With each attack, I'm learning to intentionally choose to respect who He is and believe that He cares about me in the midst of it, even if my emotions seek to persuade me that He's oblivious or unsympathetic.

Don't rush the One in control

In this biblical story, Jesus also speaks directly to the wind and sea. Although there's a difference between Matthew and Mark on whether He addresses His disciples or the storm first, both accounts clearly tell us that Jesus rebukes these forces of nature. Mark says He commands them, "Peace! Be still!" (Mark 4:39).

A "great calm," as Matthew writes in Matthew 8:26, follows. In an instance, this storm that threatened to sink their boat and drown them has been tamed by Jesus' words alone. His friends react by saying to one another, "Who then is this, that even the wind and the sea obey him?" (Mark 4:41).

Now when the disciples woke Jesus up, they obviously expected Him to do something. After all, Matthew notes that they said, "Save us, Lord" (Matt. 8:25). But from their reaction, it's clear Jesus shocked and awed them with His solution to the problem. Even after all the miracles they'd witnessed, they weren't expecting their friend and teacher to exercise authority over nature.

Jesus' dominance over the wind and sea remind me that there wasn't one moment during that voyage that He wasn't in control. He could've woken up at any point and stopped the storm. Yet, His disciples didn't pause to ask, "What would Jesus do?" Instead of patiently waiting for His timing, they frantically pushed Him to intervene in their timing, which, in their defense, I do understand. After all, their boat *was* filling up with water.

While I like to imagine that I would've responded with patience if I'd been aboard that boat with Jesus and His disciples, it's more likely I'd have spearheaded the efforts to wake Him from His nap. In situations where I feel a loss of control, my initial instinct is to act, rather than wait. I'm aware that God *can* control the "wind" and "waves" in my life, yet for some reason He's allowing them to rage on. He's not approaching my situation with the urgency that I want.

My desire to chase after control has been especially true when Ted and I have encountered unemployment. As I've written about in my book *Team Us,* in our early years of marriage, the company Ted worked for was bought out by a larger organization. In the process, he was laid off. This was the first time we experienced job loss together and it happened prior to the pink slips I'll talk about later in chapter 4.

Ted's response was to spend months contemplating what to do next. He wasn't sure whether to continue in the same field he was in or instead to pursue something entirely different. During this time, he did work as a contractor on a few short-term projects as he wrestled with the future, but I hated the ambiguity of short-term work. I wanted something permanent and stable, something *right now.* I was a stay-at-home mom at the time and urgently began to think, "If Ted isn't going to figure this out quickly and God isn't going to provide a job soon, then I'll go back to work. I'll solve this problem for us."

I didn't end up returning to a nine-to-five job. Instead, God pushed me to slowly and painfully come to terms with the fact that there were areas I simply couldn't control, including how long it took Ted to figure out his career path. I had to learn to live with ambiguity. At the same time, I was convicted to focus my attention on areas I could regulate. I *could* monitor my reactions to his indecisiveness, choosing gentleness over annoyance. I *could* pray for self-control not to push, prod, and nag Ted to find a job. And, I *could* choose to trust God—the One who was ultimately in control of Ted's employment—with our future, rather than attempting to fix it myself.

It wasn't easy to center my thoughts and my behavior on what I could control and trust God with what I couldn't. It was a daily, sometimes hourly struggle. After all, what if God didn't provide for us in what I felt was a timely manner? Would we be okay financially?

Just like the disciples, I wrestled then, and still often do now, with wanting my perfect timing to also be God's perfect timing. But this story of Jesus' calming of the wind and waves reminds me that God's timetable isn't mine to speed up. He isn't hoping that I'll solve the situation on my own and save Him the effort. Rather, His perceived tardiness provides me an opportunity to practice again and again how to relinquish control and trust my well-being to Him.

WHAT TO DO WHEN YOU FEEL OVERWHELMED

As I've written on my panic attacks and shared one-on-one about them the last several years, more and more women have responded with, "Me too." I'd never realized how many others grieved the loss of control that stems from anxiety. Maybe you're one of them. It could be that you read the beginning of this chapter and resonated with my story.

I've also talked to other women who've told me they aren't prone to panic attacks. They don't experience them. Yet what they do feel is overwhelmed at times by all the expectations, both the positive and negative, placed on them. In those moments, they too struggle with a loss of control and the frustration it brings. They find themselves in a place where they need help navigating this loss well.

Whichever tribe you resonate with, there are practical actions you can take when you feel overwhelmed. Here are a few things that have been beneficial to me.

Identify triggers

I've learned to identify those situations, environments, and emotions most likely to "trigger" or serve as a stimulus for a panic attack or cause me to feel overwhelmed. Dark, unlit spaces often leave me experiencing anxiety. Other triggers include large crowds in small spaces, situations where I feel overwhelmed by the number of expectations given me, and environments where it's difficult to keep track of my children such as a busy museum, playground, or shopping center. I do my best to avoid these triggers, but sometimes I'm simply not able to. This is when I practice the following measures.

Talk to God

The night Savannah told me she was afraid of the dark, I reminded her that suspicious shadows and unexpected creaks weren't the only thing residing in the darkness. Jesus was there too, and she could talk to Him any time. The wisdom I offered Savannah is also mine for the taking. When the panic invades or I feel overwhelmed, God is ready and willing to help me. I just need to call on Him. Most of the time, my cry is simple. A "help me" goes far. If there's anything fear is afraid of, it's Him.

Talk to myself

Once I've talked to Him, I talk to myself. Not just any words, but words of truth. I've found that memorizing Scripture passages such as Psalm 91 minister faith to me, which is the opposite of fear. In this passage, David reaffirms that God is his refuge and fortress in times of trouble. He speaks of God's protection, deliverance, and help.

Talk to others

When I'm hit with an attack or feel overwhelmed, I often call Ted or a close friend. Just as I offered words of comfort to Savannah, they also speak similar words to me. They remind me I'm not alone. They help turn my attention to God, as they walk beside me and encourage me to rely on Him. This was specifically true in the months that followed our miscarriage. Ted was laid off soon after and I hit perhaps the lowest point in my life as I entertained suicidal thoughts. I pondered what would happen if I took all of my antidepressants at once. Rather than keeping these thoughts to myself out of shame, though, a message at church challenged me to talk about them with Ted. I found freedom and accountability in doing so.

There is one caveat I have in talking to others about these feelings and struggles. I choose carefully who I confide in and pick individuals who won't make it a purely spiritual issue by telling me that I simply need more faith. It's important to trust in friends who will encourage me to view the panic from both a spiritual *and* physical perspective.

BE SOMEONE ELSE'S VILLAGE

You and I most likely have friends and family who are also grieving a loss of control. In what ways can we focus on their needs and best support them? My friend Rhonda Owens's story offers us some practical suggestions.

Rhonda knows well what it's like to be daily reminded that she's not in control of her life. In 2016, the Owenses traded a decade-long season of comfort and community to follow God on a global sailing adventure, only to discover that maybe sailing wasn't what He wanted them to do after all.

....

I must preface this story by telling you that my husband and I are sensible, sane people. We parent two lovely girls, ages fifteen and five. I am a former high school English teacher turned stay-at-home, freelance-writing mom, and my husband is a nonprofit executive who has managed and invested literally millions of dollars before choosing to go into ministry as an executive pastor and found time to coach two high school tennis teams on the side for six months out of the year.

For over a decade, we lived a happy, comfortable life in a small rural town in northwest Ohio. It's in light of this rational, balanced description that the plot thickens: in the last eight months, we have sold 95 percent of our possessions (including our house and cars), purchased a sailboat, taken sailing lessons, moved our family onto said sailboat, plotted a course to travel the world, and started a YouTube channel to document our journey as well as the stories of fellow Christian workers we'd meet along the way.

And then, complicating matters immensely, it became clear that the sailboat, like our home before it, became more like an anchor weighing us down, and that taking on the expense and maintenance of a boat was, in essence, like tethering ourselves to another anchor. Which is why (after much discussion and prayer) we decided to put the boat up for sale after a mere five months of ownership.

Of course, the first question we are asked regularly is *Why? Why would you give up the comfort and community you've worked so hard to build?*

Ultimately, our goal was to position ourselves so that God could work *through* us—we wanted to travel around the world to "shine like stars in the sky as [we] hold firmly to the word of life" (Phil. 2:15–16 NIV), and we wanted to document our journey as well as the journeys of fellow believers along the way. Our hope was to inspire others to "shine like stars" too.

But it has been the weirdest, most harrowing and unsettling thing to have positioned ourselves into a space where we thought God could work *through* us, only to find that God planned all along to use this big life change to work *on* us and *in* us, instead. God has knocked us off of the cutesy little pedestal on which we had (unwittingly and unintentionally) placed ourselves, and He's giving us a good dose of Him, which is what we've needed and longed for all along.

However, selling the boat is a big act of faith . . . because, again, what's next? The short answer is this: we don't know what's next, and what we're learning is that it's okay that we don't know. This "not knowing" isn't a surprise, now, and we're settling in to this most unsettling space, embracing the unknown next. Like a couple of kids, we've bellyached a bunch about this messy and erratic space of trying to follow the Holy Spirit's lead, but it's as if a switch kicked on and suddenly we see this time as an exciting gift where our whole family is growing exponentially beyond measure compared to pretty much any other time in our lives.

As you can imagine, these decisions—to leave a decade-long season of comfort and community, to uproot our girls from all they know, to embark on a spiritual pilgrimage for more of God—have led us into living a story that is disconcertingly valuable, unnervingly beneficial, and perplexingly worthwhile. Never mind that in comparison, this lifestyle change has us feeling like our lives are careening wildly out of control.

Rhonda says that community support has been a constant in all the uncertainty and change. The Owenses' friends and family have made it a priority to support them long-term, which has helped to ease some of the grief they've experienced in their transitions.

What has the community they left behind done to support them, and how can we do the same for people in our lives? Some things stand out.

Commit to keep in mind

The Owenses' community hasn't let the family's physical absence at church, school, dance, or Bible study result in forgetfulness. They've committed to keep the Owenses in mind. Rhonda says, "I've learned from our community that love can and will sustain and support over the miles when friends choose to reject the 'out-of-sight, out-of-mind' mentality. It has been months since we've seen anyone from our community, but their decision to continue reaching out to us has inspired me to do the same for others."

You and I can determine to do the same. Whether those we know who grieve a loss of control live in the same city or an ocean away, we can be inspired by the Owenses' community to keep them and their needs in the forefront of our minds.

Commit to pray

Consistent prayer is another way the Owenses' community has supported them. "My husband receives a text message from one friend each morning, letting him know that he is covered in prayer," Rhonda shares. Every day, they are reminded that their friends and family back home not only think of them, but are asking God to protect and provide for them.

Just like the Owenses' community, we can not only commit to pray, but we can determine to let those we're praying for know that we are. Sometimes a short text or quick phone call that confirms we are indeed interceding for them makes a big difference as someone grieves a loss of control.

Commit to encourage

A third way we can offer support is through active, practical encouragement. The Owenses' community has been intentional to do this. Rhonda says, "One of my friends organized a calendar where she scheduled fifty-two friends—one per week—to not only pray for our family, but also to send Scripture and words of encouragement to us. We've been randomly gifted with inspirational devotionals and books via our Kindle."

Their support hasn't been confined to Rhonda and her husband. "My oldest daughter has had numerous video chats, text messages, emails, and letters from friends," Rhonda shares. "Her youth pastor, prior to our departure, prepared an entire box of letters for her—one to open on her first day of the boat, her thirtieth day on the boat, her ninetieth day on the boat, etc.—so that she will continue to have over a year of encouraging words from a person who spiritually impacts her in ways my husband and I cannot. Even our five-year-old has been blessed with short video messages from her friends via texts and hand-drawn pictures sent along in the mail."

> **While our lives are busy, it doesn't demand a lot of us to share a Scripture verse, write a handwritten note, treat someone to coffee or tea.**

While our lives are busy, it doesn't demand a lot of us to share a Scripture verse, write a handwritten note, treat someone to coffee or tea, or send a care package. Sometimes small efforts lift someone's spirits in large, significant ways, reminding them that they aren't alone in what they face.

THE SLOW WEAN OF CONTROL

In 2010, Savannah celebrated her second birthday. With this changing of age came the dreaded season of pacifier weaning. She grieved hard the loss of her precious "Night Night," as she called it, and fought fiercely for the control to keep it.

I understood. It had only been a few months since our miscarriage. I knew how difficult it was to face an unexpected change that rendered me powerless. While saying goodbye to a pacifier wasn't the same as the death of a child, I empathized with Savannah. I saw my pain in hers.

One day, as she sat on the couch screaming, "Night Night!" at me, I remained beside her. I offered comfort, but didn't stop her pain by returning the pacifier. Instead, I allowed her to grieve the loss of the item and the loss of control, helping her process with my presence and my empathy. And, because of the relationship we've built, she felt the freedom to run to my arms and cry and yell within my embrace.

In my own loss, God has done for me what I sought to do for Savannah. He hasn't removed my sorrow. Most of the time, He doesn't even return what I've lost. What He does do is remain beside me. He allows me to grieve, comforting me with His presence and His empathy. And, because of the relationship we've built, I feel the freedom to run to His arms and cry and yell within His embrace. I love what author, speaker, and quadriplegic Joni Eareckson Tada writes. She says:

> God, like a father, doesn't just give advice. He gives himself. He becomes the husband to the grieving widow (Isaiah 54:5). He becomes the comforter to the barren woman (Isaiah 54:1). He becomes the father of the orphaned (Psalm 10:14). He becomes the bridegroom to the single person (Isaiah 62:5). He is the healer to the sick (Exodus 15:26). He is the wonderful counselor to the confused and depressed (Isaiah 9:6).
>
> This is what you do when someone you love is in anguish; you respond to the plea of their heart by giving them your

heart. If you are the One at the center of the universe, holding it together, if everything moves, breathes, and has its being in you, you can do no more than give yourself (Acts 17:28).[1]

As you grieve your own seasons of loss of control, may you too feel the freedom to run to His arms and cry and yell within His embrace. I promise He's ready and willing to receive you.

And may you also offer your presence, your empathy, and your embrace to those around you who, like Savannah, grieve their own loss and mourn a sense of control they once had. Because, just as there is nothing greater God can give us than Himself, there's nothing greater we can give others than our willingness to brave their sorrow with them.

CHAPTER 2

RELATIONSHIPS

*"To love at all is to be vulnerable. Love anything and your
heart will be wrung and possibly broken."*
— C. S. Lewis[1]

Throughout my childhood, an avocado-green, crushed velvet-covered loveseat proudly stood in my Grandpa and Grandma Schmidt's living room. It unashamedly screamed 1970s, akin to décor one might see in a rerun of *The Brady Bunch*. None of us grandkids cared, though, if it was dated by a decade or two. This blast from my grandparents' pre-grandkid past was *the* coveted place to sit. Not only was it soft, but it rocked. In those younger, more carefree days of mine, we'd all squeeze onto it, about as organized as monkeys in a barrel, and we would rock and rock.

When I grew up, got married, and had a couple babies of my own, the day came when the childhood joy of rocking on this loveseat was darkened by the adult realization of what a terrible foe Alzheimer's disease is.

I remember it well. It was 2006. My grandpa, the jovial, generous man whose smile warms my earliest memories, had battled heart problems for several years. As hard as he fought, his heart continued to weaken, his strength slowly waned, and he said goodbye to us.

When I reflect on his last days, I tenderly recall the phone calls that connected the two of us despite our differing time zones and the five-state distance that separated us. While I couldn't hold his hand or catch a glimpse of his grin one last time, it comforted me to know that photographs of my newly born, second daughter, Ava, hung in his hospital room and brought his spirit joy even as his body failed him.

At the news of his death, Ted, our daughters, and I traveled from our home in Colorado Springs to the small lake town in Ohio my parents had grown up in to attend his funeral. We brought with us fifty copies of a memorial book we'd created to hand out at the service. That day, as I sat on that avocado-green, crushed velvet-covered loveseat once more, I watched my grandma look at this collection of photos and family memories for the first time.

My grandpa died during the early stages of her Alzheimer's disease, before it hit Grandma full force.

Her response was not what I expected, and it was far from what I'd hoped.

Where recognition and remembrance should have been, there stood unfamiliarity and confusion. "He was a good man?" she questioned, her uncertainty painfully evident.

"Oh, yes," Ted told her.

His response didn't seem to calm her. Deep concern continued to etch itself across her face.

"Were we . . . um," she hesitated, nervously. "Married?" As someone who understood her deeply religious upbringing and was aware of the years she had served alongside my grandpa as a pastor's wife, her underlying fear was obvious. She was worried that they'd lived together, out of wedlock.

"Yes, you were," I gently assured her. "You were married for fifty-two years."

In that moment, though, those fifty-two years had tragically faded from her memory. She didn't know they'd happened. Her wedding lived on only in pictures and the stories of others.

My grandpa died during the early stages of her Alzheimer's disease, before it hit Grandma full force. Following his death, my parents sacrificially cared for her and sought to navigate the unknown territory of dementia well. In the beginning, she lived with them, but as Grandma's condition worsened, my parents made the tough decision to move her to an assisted living group home.

Memories of her earthly years continued to vanish for her. On those few times I was able to visit, she knew I cared about her, but she didn't know who I was. She's forgotten decades of Scrabble games, the summer weeks I'd faithfully spent at her house, and how much she loved taking me out to eat. She couldn't recall the significance of my relationship with her, and there was absolutely nothing I could do to restore that.

HUMANITY'S FIRST BREAKUP

Most of us have grieved the loss of a relationship. We've felt the pain of knowing that someone we love is still living his or her life, but our role in it has faded and may even be nonexistent. It could be an estranged family member, a friend who pulls away, a divorce, or as with my grandma, the loss of connection as a result of dementia.

The relational losses I've grieved over the years have led me to reflect on the earliest story of connection severed, to the series of disastrous decisions made by our very, very, *very* great-grandparents, Adam and Eve, and recorded in the first pages of the Bible. It's in this biblical account that we're told the story of what I like to call "humanity's first breakup." It's the narrative of how the relationship between God and humans was shattered.

Genesis opens with the creation. Light is peeled away from darkness. Earth takes form and grows vegetation. Fish, birds, and land animals spring to life. God uses words to create, speaking each of these into existence. Yet when it comes time for Him to make humans, the Bible tells us that He takes a different approach. He gets crafty.

And I'm not talking crafty in the cunning, sly, or devious sort of way. Nope, I mean He literally gets His hands dirty in a Saturday-morning, PBS-pottery-show fashion. He comes down to earth and forms Adam from dust. It's from this that God skillfully molds a rib cage, limbic system, spleen, corneas, and all the other wonders of the human body that scientists still marvel at today. He doesn't stop there, though. He does what, to my knowledge, no Saturday-morning, PBS-pottery show has ever attempted. God takes a lifeless form made from dirt, breathes His own breath into it, and brings forth a soul, a spirit.

God's intricate care of Adam isn't finished with body and soul. He doesn't animate this first man and simply wish him luck. There's no, "Break a leg, Adam. Remember, it's survival of the fittest out there." Rather, the Author of Adam's story provides him with a garden home, backyard-to-table cuisine, and the companionship of a wife, Eve. God offers this couple His friendship, His fellowship, and His trust. Physically, emotionally, spiritually, and relationally, they lack nothing.

If any story should have had a fairy-tale ending, *this* was it. But it didn't.

You may remember that in this perfect garden where humans commune closely with God, there is one caveat, only one rule God wants this first family to follow. It involves the strictly off-limit fruit of a solitary tree—the Tree of the Knowledge of Good and Evil. And it's at this tree that Satan, in the form of a serpent, convinces Eve to question God's goodness and to distrust His motives. He persuades her that God is selfishly withholding knowledge from her, and that if she eats of the fruit of this tree, she'll be wise just like God.

Here's where Eve makes the first of many disastrous decisions and takes a bite, offering one to Adam too. This treason results in more poor choices. Adam and Eve hide themselves in leafy shame from

God, rather than take responsibility for their actions. When they're discovered, they choose to blame the serpent, each other, and even God Himself for their defiance.

With this, Adam and Eve usher in humanity's very first breakup. And ever since, their descendants, which include you and me, have dealt with relational strife, brokenness, and loss.

WHEN THE HEART DOESN'T FEEL LIKE IT CAN GO ON

I was a sophomore in college when I first determined that marriage wasn't for me. While I'd love to say this declaration of mine stemmed from logical reasoning or God-given direction, it didn't. Its kindling was romantic deception and disloyalty set aflame by the agonizing heartbreak I felt in the wake of their discovery.

"I cheated on you," came the telephone confession, offered to me over the two-thousand plus miles of Pacific Ocean that separated California from Hawaii. I'd been in a long-distance relationship for the past eight months, one that had developed from a two-year-long friendship prior to my move. We were nearing what was supposed to be his turn to buy an airline ticket, hop on a plane, and visit me.

His turn never came.

My mind frantically grasped to make sense of these four words, as I angrily demanded the details of who, what, where, and when. Yet, what I really wanted to know was

I assumed the flagrant red flags of consistent dishonesty and his disinterest in pursuing a growing relationship with Jesus would change with time, and with me.

"why?" It was the one haunting question to which, even years later when we would meet again and I'd be given a genuine apology, I never received a satisfactory answer.

I'm not sure why I'd expected this relationship to endure, let alone end any differently. He and I weren't a good fit, and I knew it. In fact, I'd even felt the Holy Spirit gently prompt me not to date him, but I believed I knew better. I assumed the flagrant red flags of consistent dishonesty and his disinterest in pursuing a growing relationship with Jesus would change with time, and with me.

They didn't.

As I soon realized, a long-distance breakup is a double-edged sword. On one hand, I didn't fear accidentally running into him or seeing him with another woman. There were no favorite date night spots to litter the drive to work or to school. I didn't have to map out new routes or avoid certain haunts. On the other hand, there was also a severe, crippling lack of closure and a tormenting sense that I hadn't been given the full story. The physical distance kept me from being able to discern fact from fiction.

After our breakup, I had mutual friends tell me he'd been dating someone else while we were still supposedly together. More casual friends told me that he'd kept our long-distance relationship a secret from them. They had no clue we'd dated seriously. I even began to wonder if maybe he hadn't cheated in the manner he confessed to, but instead had fabricated the story to manipulate *me* into breaking up with *him*; that it was his cowardly way of ending the long-distance relationship. I didn't know who or what to believe.

When I wasn't working my part-time job or in class, I retreated to my room at my parents' house and listened to the same cheesy love song over and over again. The repetitive sounds of Celine Dion's "My Heart Will Go On" echoed hour after hour from behind my closed door. It simultaneously calmed and tormented me. In response, my mom offered me handwritten cards of comfort, while my sisters silently worried.

I stopped eating and my clothes grew looser and looser. Even my boss noticed the change. She too attempted to soothe my broken heart, yet there weren't any magic words to ease the pain. Nobody's story of "I went through a breakup and survived" helped. It was a relational loss unlike any I'd experienced before, and one from which it would take me at least a year to finally move on.

WHEN GOD FILLS OUR RELATIONAL BROKENNESS WITH HOPE

My friend Allison (names have been changed) also knows well the pain of relational brokenness, although in this particular case, it's not the romantic kind. She grieves not having a strong, close-knit relationship with her mom.

"For many reasons, my relationship with my mom didn't make the leap between adolescence and adulthood," she told me. "Because it's a death of relationship but not a death of love, it's been difficult to accept and even more difficult to grieve. Both of us have tried various resuscitation techniques without success."

But Allison's narrative doesn't stop there. There's more to her story. Even though her relationship with her mom hasn't thrived, God has provided for Allison in other ways. In the midst of her ongoing grief, He's brought much-needed and perfectly timed friendships into her life. She shares:

....

The word *mentor* wasn't part of my personal dictionary when I first met Kim. She was fifteen years older than me, asked wonderful questions, and seemed to enjoy my answers. It was through her gentle leading and listening that I found support in the early years of marriage and parenting. When relationships felt hopeless, she offered up her own story as evidence of God's never-ending ability to sustain.

Over time, a part of Kim also became part of me—a sameness that wasn't genetic, but spiritual. I became confident I could invest in others in the same way she invested in me—a domino effect of spiritual mothering. While the years have found us busier with ministry and life and family, God used this woman to show me what healthy relationships between women might become.

The second woman entered my life almost a decade later. Tracy and I met in a professional sense, but from her first email I sensed there was something more. We met during a time when my mom and I were on an extended communication sabbatical, one that would last nearly three years. I was busy raising kids while constructing a career and serving in ministry alongside my husband, all of which kept the dull ache of loneliness for my mom manageable. But God wasn't looking for manageable; He was looking to be invited into the ache.

The Lord used Tracy to teach me about the Holy Spirit and the intimacy available through His indwelling presence. She was both sensitive to God and strong in her relationships. Tracy had beautiful, Spirit-led boundaries as she invited others into her life while refusing to be trampled by unhealthy people. I learned the Spirit was gentle and empowering—a whisper and a roar. And I invited His Spirit to live through me in exactly that way.

....

It's this community that has helped Allison attempt to grieve her loss well. The willingness of Kim and Tracy to live life alongside her and encourage in the way a mother would has inspired Allison to continually choose hope instead of bitterness. She says:

....

Because two women took the time to love me and hear me, I've learned to wrap the pain in peace. At the end of our lives here on earth, my mom and I are both daughters of God and we will spend our lives together eternally—free of conflict, full of acceptance. If this is the relationship God gives us, then I choose to be forever grateful.

But for now—here on earth—I'm reminded of God's unrelenting love for me as He refuses to leave me alone. I feel His love through the presence of healthy relationships, as both Kim's and Tracy's gentle steering of conversation and attitudes have kept me from falling facedown in a pool of bitterness. By sharing their stories, they highlighted the beauty of my own.

....

While Allison's words remind you and me how important friendship is as we grieve loss, I've found that sometimes seeking out and diving into community is difficult. It's often even more difficult when we've suffered a relational loss such as my breakup or Allison's strained connection with her mom. Just as Adam and Eve hid in the garden, our natural tendency can be to hide when we're mourning a broken relationship, even if that hiding is from people who haven't hurt us. Relational loss and the devastating hurt it inflicts can cause us to pull away, to draw back, and to isolate ourselves from others. It's one reason my college self determined not to get married. I was terrified of the vulnerability required and the potential heartbreak it might bring.

Yet how can you and I honestly level with ourselves in the midst of our pain and tell if we've chosen isolation over community, and perhaps aren't even admitting it to ourselves? One of my favorite films offers insight.

Will I choose to engage in genuine, deep relationships with others even after I've been hurt?

HOW TO TELL IF YOU'RE A RELATIONAL REFUGEE

On December 31, 1941, Warner Bros. Pictures' producer Hal Wallis sent an interoffice memo letting all departments know of the title change on a current project. He wrote, "The story we recently purchased entitled 'Everybody Comes to Rick's' will hereafter be known as . . . 'Casablanca'."[2] This newly named work premiered almost a year later in New York City and, ever since, critics and moviegoers alike have had a beautiful, enduring friendship with it. But what is it about *Casablanca* that made it so successful, not only in the 1940s, but even now?

Under all the technical and artistic excellence that's made this film a classic for over seventy years, there's a timeless truth that the characters in this film illustrate for me every single time I watch it. They demonstrate that common people like you and me have the capacity to choose how we bear the searing, and sometimes lifelong, scars of relational loss. *Casablanca* challenges me to consider: Will I choose to engage in genuine, deep relationships with others even after I've been hurt? Or will I—like the film's protagonist Rick Blaine—spend a part of my life as a relational refugee?

Casablanca is a story of refugees. In this World War II–set drama, Europeans are fleeing their home countries and desperately trying to reach Lisbon, Portugal, which serves as a port of exit to America. Unfortunately, getting to Lisbon is no easy feat. As a result, it's in French-controlled Morocco that these immigrants do anything they can to obtain travel visas that will get them to Lisbon, and eventually to the States. Some are fortunate, but many aren't and find themselves indefinitely stranded in the city of Casablanca.

In this city of refugees, we're introduced to Rick, played by Humphrey Bogart. He's a no-nonsense American who runs a busy bar and casino named Rick's Café Américain. Rick is, as the *New York Times*'s original 1942 review of the film states, the "cool, cynical, efficient and super-wise guy who operates his business strictly for profit but has a core of sentiment and idealism inside."[3] Yet it's this core of sentiment and idealism that he's hesitant to display.

What's his motivation for keeping those he regularly interacts with at arm's length? Two words: relational loss.

Rick's heart was broken by a woman of intrigue he'd fallen deeply in love with while in Paris, and it's this relational agony, this loss, that results in the sarcastic, aloof man we're introduced to in *Casablanca*. We come to see that Rick isn't just a political refugee, seeking safety from the Nazi regime, but he's also a relational refugee. He flees emotional connection and vulnerability for the protection of independence, isolation, and bourbon.

Sometimes I do the same thing. I isolate myself from personal connection in an effort to protect my heart from further pain. For me, it's often easy to react to relational hurt and loss with withdrawal. I may not display it by being aloof and detached, as Rick does. Instead, I may mask it with humor that keeps all my interactions at a surface level. Or, it could be that I keep myself so busy that I have a constant excuse for not engaging others in a deep, meaningful manner.

How can you tell if, like Rick and me, you've allowed grief to cause you to become a relational refugee too? Let's look at some principles that Rick lives by. See if you recognize yourself in any of them.

I align myself with no one

Rick is fiercely independent to the point that interdependence, or the action of being in a "mutually reliant"[4] relationship, isn't a dynamic he seeks out. He purposely chooses not to align himself with anyone or anything in a meaningful manner.

Now most of us don't practice this idea of non-allegiance in our everyday lives as blatantly as Rick does. We don't go around brashly and directly declaring our independence. Instead, our proclamation is more subtle, maybe even at times passive-aggressive.

In my daily life, it happens most often in my marriage. (Obviously, I eventually changed my mind about never getting married.) If you're married, or have been married, you understand that as fulfilling as marriage can be, husbands (and wives) will deeply disappoint at times. It happens.

Because of Ted's demanding work schedule, a common issue in

our relationship is that sometimes he commits to do something for me and then for reasons often outside of his control, he can't. I should be understanding, and there are times that I am. But there are also times, more frequent than I care to admit, when I'm hurt and even offended. I allow the sting of disappointment to make me shun the interdependence Ted and I are meant to have. In its place, I favor independence. "That's okay," I stoically say, frustration in my voice. "I'll just do it myself." What's worse is it doesn't stop there. Days after the initial letdown, I still operate on my own. "I won't ask Ted to help me," I tell myself. "I'll do it myself. I doubt he even has time." Self-pity and self-protection drive me to avoid the possibility of future disappointment and to isolate myself. It's a lonely place to retreat to and wounds our relationship.

Maybe you can relate. When faced with a problem, is it ever your first instinct to determine that you can deal with it better and more safely on your own, rather than share your burden? If you find yourself shying away from interdependence in relationships for self-dependence, then you may want to step back and consider if you've allowed past or current hurt to drive you to isolation. It's possible you have.

I stick my neck out for nobody

One of Rick's famous lines is, "I stick my neck out for nobody!" In this statement, he clearly communicates: I don't get involved in any problems that aren't my own. I don't risk my comfort, safety, or reputation to help others. I too have thought this and at times even uttered a similar sentiment, albeit on a much smaller scale than Rick.

I'm a fundraiser softy. If a friend, family member, or even acquaintance is raising money for medical bills, adoption, classroom supplies, or a mission trip, I'm 95 percent likely to donate, depending on our current financial situation. I'll even order a shirt that I never intend to wear if it's for a worthy cause. The truth is, whenever I'm fiscally able, I love to give. Growing up, my parents modeled generosity for me and it's a practice I try to model for my kids. For me, giving is fun . . . most of the time.

Something happened last spring, though, that caused me to become cynical about it for the first time in my life.

Olivia and Ava planned to perform with a group at Carnegie Hall in New York City that June, and they both had solos. Those of you who have kids involved in any activity that includes travel, such as baseball, band or, like us, theater and dance, know it's expensive. We decided to ask our community for help. Rather than go with a standard online pledge campaign, we got creative and organized an online auction. We invited all of our family and friends, both locally and around the country, to bid.

Great idea. Right? Huge success. Yes? No. It was an utter failure. We received a grand total of three bids.

I was deflated, disappointed, and bitterly jaded. Sure, there was no obvious relational loss, but I was worn out and wearied by the lack of support I felt. Where was our community? Why weren't they financially cheering us on? While my past giving was motivated by a desire to help and not a sense of future quid pro quo, I started to question why I kept sticking out my financial neck for others. Maybe I'd be better off holding on to our money and exclusively funding only our kids' activities. My thoughts, attitude, and even some of my frustrated confessions to Ted became that of "I stick my neck out for nobody."

Have you ever had a similar mindset as you grieve relational loss or a lack of support from others? It may be that you remember the ways you helped and supported a person with whom you're either no longer in relationship or your interactions are strained. Perhaps you stuck your neck out for them and now you regret it. If you find yourself reluctant and unwilling to help others for fear of being hurt again or unsupported, you may have isolated yourself.

Community has let me down in the past and it will again

Rick may facilitate community in his bar, but he doesn't engage in it. Yes, he knows some people, spends time with others, and has conversations, but he doesn't let anyone know much about him. Not even his good buddy, Sam. He keeps his relationship with patrons, and even those who consider him a friend, more shallow. For Rick, vulnerability with others equals hurt.

Earlier in our marriage, Ted and I lived in Colorado Springs. We'd been there almost two years after moving cross-country from Virginia. Olivia and Ava were in the preschool and toddler phases, and our two youngest daughters had yet to be born. At our previous church in Virginia, we'd been active in small groups, but we had yet to get involved in one at our church in Colorado. We decided that needed to change, so we joined one that advertised itself as "kid friendly." It met on Sunday nights, included a potluck dinner, and the parents took turns with childcare duty. We had no family in town and no good babysitter, so it was a perfect fit. Our reality was: no childcare meant no small group.

The first month or two went well. Fantastic, even . . . or so we believed. We met new couples and built new friendships. But then, one Sunday night, it happened. We unexpectedly discovered that our small family was *the* elephant in the small-group room. The issue of childcare in this kid-friendly group was broached. Several couples expressed their dissatisfaction with the child-watching system. They argued that their kids were in elementary school and didn't need supervision. They could entertain themselves or sit quietly beside them. Because of this, they didn't want to take a turn on childcare duty, and they certainly didn't want to contribute money toward hiring a weekly babysitter to watch all the kids. Ted and I slowly realized that, aside from the small-group leaders whose youngest was two and could be watched by older siblings, we were the only couple exclusively with small children. While no one uttered the name "Slater," we knew that our kids—who, for the record, were well behaved— were the issue about which everyone else was complaining. Yet no one would directly say it. The resentment expressed was communicated in an indirect, passive-aggressive fashion.

I left small group that night angry, disillusioned, and hurt. We had boldly jumped into this gathering, longing to develop deep connections with other couples from our church, only to be disappointed over childcare. I wondered if these couples had even stopped to contemplate our position. Did they consider that the current childcare system was what allowed us to show up each time, or were they too focused on their own needs and desires to do so?

As a result, we became disenchanted, small-group dropouts. It took several years before we braved another one, and that required relocation to a different state and membership at a different church. This one bad, wounding experience within community left me for years fearful of being hurt again in that context.

If you're choosing to distance yourself and not participate in some form of community, whether with a close friend or a group, you may be isolating yourself.

What about you? Are you afraid that community will let you down too because it has in the past? The truth is we've all been there. We've all been let down by others, and the pain of previous relational loss can make this letdown feel even bigger. If you're choosing to distance yourself and not participate in some form of community, whether with a close friend or a group, you may be isolating yourself. Which, I suppose, is cool if you're Bogart. But, as I've learned, not if you're an off-screen personality like me.

GRIEVING RELATIONAL LOSS WELL

Did you identify at all with Rick or with me? Maybe you've realized that you're a full-fledged relational refugee too, or perhaps you only see yourself in one of the principles he lived by. Whatever the case may be, I've learned there are steps you and I can take to better walk through loss in a community-inclusive way.

It's healthy to acknowledge and grieve loss

First things first: grieve. Go ahead and do it. Mourn deeply your loss. I do. Don't attempt to be stronger than you are and pretend the deterioration or loss of a relationship doesn't bother you. Think back to Allison's story. She first shared that, yes, she grieves not having a strong connection with her mom. She doesn't deny that the pain of this severed bond exists.

I'm learning that in order to grieve a loss, we have to choose to process our feelings in a healthy way. If you need to cry—weep even—allow yourself to do so. That really is okay. Processing may also involve confiding in a trusted friend or professional counselor. For me, the hardest struggle with this is to be mindful that I don't allow my confiding to become destructive venting. I have to keep in mind these words from author Suzanne Hadley Gosselin:

> The term "venting" sounds deceptively therapeutic. The truth is, venting involves voicing frustrations that are often damaging to a person or a cause. By giving ourselves permission to "vent," we allow words to pour out unchecked, taking little time to consider whether they're gossip, slander or just good, old-fashioned complaint.
>
> I can think of times when I have listened to a friend "vent" only to walk away with a diminished view of a person or ministry. The enemy seems to use such unrestrained moments to stall and discredit God's work, and even mire a believer in sin. Proverbs 10:19 says, "When words are many, sin is not absent, but he who holds his tongue is wise."[5]

The idea here is that haphazard grieving results in additional relational carnage, while mindful grieving results in freedom. When you and I carefully grieve our loss with purpose and intention, it allows us to more freely and vulnerably interact with others. Why? Because self-protection mode, whether we realize it or not, inhibits our ability to connect in meaningful ways. So, as I said, grieve. Go ahead and do it, just be wise in the manner.

It's healing to pray for the other person

With relational loss, comes hurt. It may stem from being rejected, betrayed, or disappointed. Whether you and I admit it or not, if we aren't careful this hurt can easily harden into a lack of forgiveness, or even deep-seated bitterness. That's why praying for the other person is important. Here's the thing about prayer: It softens *our* hearts. It changes *us*.

It's not easy to pray for someone who has hurt or abandoned us, though. I'm currently in a situation that requires I pray for several individuals who've been unkind to one of my daughters, and encourage her to do the same. Forcing myself to personally do this, let alone instruct her to do so, is excruciatingly difficult. Most of the time, I don't want to. I even have my moments where I tell God that I simply can't. It's painful and humiliating to ask Him to bless those whom I'd rather see corrected. Yet, it's the very thing that Jesus asks us to do. He says, "Bless those who curse you. Pray for those who hurt you" (Luke 6:28 NLT). The more you and I force ourselves to consistently do this, the easier it'll become.

When we choose to pray for someone who's hurt us, God not only helps us forgive, but as He does, He begins to ease the pain. I won't lie, it's a slow process and it's certainly not a miraculous one. In my life, I've found again and again that the pain never fully goes away. Even as it fades, a tender ache remains. Yet, as we allow God to slowly soften and change us, there's the potential for a rebirth of hope that can inspire us to seek out community, rather than run from it.

It's okay to fill the relational void

When there's an estrangement, specifically from a parent, a sibling, or another family member, it may seem disloyal to seek out a mentor or friend to fill that void. Please know, it's not, although it may feel awkward at first. Just as Allison discovered, the love, care, and friendship of someone who either formally or informally steps into that role in our lives can offer the strength and support we need to grieve well.

There is one exception to this idea of filling a relational void. While it may be obvious, I feel it's worth mentioning. If you're married and grieve a lack of either emotional or physical intimacy, it's not okay to seek out fulfillment with someone else. Rather, ask for help from a trusted mentor couple, your pastor and his wife, or a professional counselor who can help you and your husband find hope and healing in your marriage. In those instances when Ted and I have struggled to remain connected, we are very careful where and in whom we seek counsel and support.

CHOOSE TO BE GOOD TO EACH OTHER IN GRIEF

It's been years since I spent long hours immersed in C. S. Lewis's The Chronicles of Narnia, but I did recently revisit my favorite of its books, *The Magician's Nephew*. And in it, I discovered what I believe is an important nugget of truth when it comes to loss.

In this story, Lewis narrates the genesis of Narnia, the world we all come to associate with Lucy, Edmund, Peter, and Susan. We discover that before these four children entered this magical land through the wardrobe, there is a boy named Digory. Tragically, Digory's mother is dying, and he desperately hopes that the great lion Aslan, the creator of Narnia, can do something to change that.

> "But please, please—won't you—can't you give me something that will cure Mother?" Up till then he had been looking at the Lion's great feet and the huge claws on them; now, in his despair, he looked up at its face. What he saw surprised him as much as anything in his whole life. For the tawny face was bent down near his own and (wonders of wonders) great shining tears stood in the Lion's eyes. They were such big, bright

tears compared with Digory's own that for a moment he felt as if the Lion must really be sorrier about his mother than he was himself.

"My son, my son," said Aslan. "I know. Grief is great. Only you and I in this land know that yet. Let us be good to one another."[6]

Did you catch what Aslan says to Digory? I mean, *really* catch it? Because when I did, I felt the need to read it multiple times.

Grief is great. Let us be good to one another.

Like I did, stop reading for moment, and linger on those two sentences. They're important. *Really* important.

With them, Lewis offers us simple, yet powerful relational wisdom that you and I can be quick to live out in times of grief: *be good to one another.*

My daughter Savannah does this instinctively. She notices someone hurting and immediately acts with empathy and compassion. Just yesterday, she heard me crying as I grieved a relational loss. Her response was to grab construction paper, scissors, tape, and markers to make me a card. She sensed that my grief was great and she was good to me, without me having to ask her to be. In that moment, I felt deeply loved. And, even though her kindness didn't erase my pain, it did remind me that I wasn't alone or forgotten.

Chances are you aren't currently in the throes of intense relational loss, but you know someone who is. It may be a loss that you can relate to. It could be that you've walked through something similar and have no problem saying, "Me too." But perhaps that's not the case. How can you respond to a relational loss with which you don't have personal experience? How can you, like Savannah, be *good* to that person?

I'm discovering that it's actually fairly simple: you and I can turn to the wisdom of those who *do* know.

For me, one such loss is divorce. Even though I have experienced a breakup, I don't know what the death of a marriage feels like. Yet I have friends and acquaintances who understand the loss well. Just in the last few years, several women I know have walked through painful divorces. They've grieved the death of their marriages and had to figure out what life looks like as a single mom. I asked two of these women if they'd be willing to share a few things they needed and wanted from their family and friends as they grieved. For the sake of anonymity, I'll call them "Michelle" and "Jennifer." Here's what they said.

Love without conditions

Sometimes it's our natural tendency to want to judge a situation and the people involved, whether it's a divorce, painful breakup, or extended-family divide, and decide if we feel they deserve our sympathy and support. Too often, many of us want to love *with* conditions, but that's not what others need from us. And, the truth is, we don't often have enough information to even accurately do that. Instead, we can be good to them by loving *without* conditions. This is exactly what both Jennifer and Michelle told me they needed as they walked through their divorces.

"A listening ear without judgment can be such a blessing," Jennifer wrote me in an email. "I was fortunate to have several close friends in whom I could confide. Despite my initial response to tell one friend, 'No, you don't need to drive here. I'll be fine,' she wouldn't take no for an answer and drove twelve hours straight just to be here for me in person right after my husband had confessed to me by email his lies and infidelities over the course of our seventeen-year marriage. She stayed for a few days and we cried together, laughed together, and prayed together, staying up until the wee hours of the morning. It was just what I needed to get through the initial shock of it all. I'm so grateful for what she did and to have her as my friend."

Unfortunately, Michelle had a different experience. As we chatted over the phone, my heart broke as she shared, "Everyone I thought was my friend just literally disappeared." She went on to explain that once many of her Christian friends learned she'd been sexually active outside of marriage after her divorce, she felt like they—with the exception of her pastor, who she says listened without judgment—"completely backed away from me and my family. They didn't know how to help, so they just disappeared." And when they did communicate with her, it seemed only to bring correction. Michelle felt discouraged, hurt, and abandoned by those she knew who claimed to love Jesus. She says what would have helped her the most was to have people "just love" her regardless of whether or not they agreed with her decisions.

Ask the right questions

Both Jennifer and Michelle told me that asking the *right* questions is important. It can help determine whether someone feels loved or feels judged. If you and I haven't experienced a particular relational loss, though, we may not know what the right questions are to even ask. It turns out it's not as difficult as it may seem.

Jennifer noted, "For those of us who don't use social media to air our personal grievances, something like divorce is kept close to the vest. However, if you know your friend is going through something, ask them about it in spite of how awkward you may feel. To them, it shows that you care and allows them to open up to you as much or as little as they would like." And, as you ask, be careful not to make assumptions. "Don't assume that you know the full story, and certainly don't judge," Jennifer added. "I've heard many people say that in a divorce, both parties are to blame. That is not always the case, so don't make assumptions. In some instances, friends heard or thought, perhaps, I was going through a divorce, but rather than ask me about it, they just kept their distance, which left me feeling judged and even more abandoned and alone."

Michelle also told me that she felt that many of her Christian friends focused on asking the wrong questions. They appeared so fixated on attempting to keep her accountable in her behavior, that they didn't ask things she really needed like, "How can we help you with the kids today?" or "Can I run to the grocery store for you?" She says she ended up finding "solace in non-Christians because they didn't care what I did. They were just like, 'You need help,' so they would come over and help me clean."

Encourage and include

When a friend or family member gets divorced, there's the temptation to feel awkward when it comes to get-togethers, holidays, or birthday parties. Should we ask a single mom and her kids to come to a party populated with married couples and their children? Or will that make them feel out of place? Jennifer and Michelle both told me that they still wanted to be included.

> **Unfortunately, for her, the invitations stopped coming after her divorce.**

Jennifer shared, "A divorced single parent may not have as much time or money to be able to socialize or participate in extracurricular activities, but do invite them to do things. Invite her to sit with you at church, go to lunch, attend your Bible study, or see a movie and then, if she needs to talk, listen. If you're totally swamped and can't go out with her, send her a quick text or an encouraging song title just to let her know that you're thinking of her. Even stopping by to give her a small bouquet of cheerful flowers from the local market can help her feel loved. The tiniest outreach can mean so much! My twelve-hour–drive friend sent me a number of encouraging song titles during and in the days and weeks following her visit. I quickly looked them up and downloaded them. They were encouraging and cathartic and helped me to focus on the Lord and the blessings He produced out of my marriage, namely my two wonderful kids."

Michelle also told me that being included would have made her feel loved and supported. Unfortunately, for her, the invitations stopped coming after her divorce. This added to the pain she and her children were already feeling. "We used to be invited places when I was married, and then when I was no longer married, it was like nobody knew how to fit me in. They didn't know how to talk to me, they didn't know what to do with me, and it hurt my children. My kids thought that because their dad left, it meant everybody was gone now because we were considered a broken family. That we're less than everyone else and, therefore, we didn't get to be invited to the cookouts, or Easter egg hunts, or anything for that matter."

These three things that Jennifer and Michelle shared that they needed and wanted, aren't reserved solely for women who've experienced a divorce. They can be applied to anyone you and I know who is mourning. So who in our lives is currently grieving a loss? This week, let's both make a mental list of one or two people and determine to take time to be good to them. Let's actively think of ways we can love them without conditions, ask the right questions, and encourage and include them.

THE ONE THING NO RELATIONAL LOSS CAN STEAL

It would seem that in my grandma's battle against dementia, that Alzheimer's won.

It assaulted the relational history and connection that once existed with her children, and their children, and their children's children. It fought its fiercest to lay waste to the connection that was slowly grown in our family over time, and it was victorious on many counts.

Yet, as I reflect on her last year of life, I gently encourage myself to think of it differently. I compel myself not to view it with such bitterness. Hatred, even.

I remind myself that as great a foe as Alzheimer's was, there was one thing it couldn't steal from Grandma, no matter how hard it tried.

Grandma never forgot her love for and faith in Jesus. It only grew stronger. She would spend her time reading her Bible and singing old

Sunday school favorites. While her relationship with us had changed, the bond she had with her Savior endured. Grandma remembered the One whose face she would soon see. Even though it isn't true for everyone stricken with this terrible disease, Grandma never forgot her love for and faith in Jesus.

The same can be true for us, if we let it. No matter what relational loss you and I carry, no matter how excruciatingly painful it is to face, we too can determine to hold on fiercely to our love for and faith in Jesus. We can brave our sorrow and, as we do, we can be good to one another too. We can choose to cry, and to love, and to live, together.

CHAPTER 3

HOME

"Home is the nicest word there is."
— Laura Ingalls Wilder[1]

"D o you miss home?" Ted asked.

"No," I replied, perhaps too quickly, and too honestly even. I added, "No place really feels like home right now."

He nodded in agreement. He understood.

It was June 2016 and we were three days into a trip to New York City, staying on the tenth floor of a Holiday Inn Express in Manhattan, within a block or two of Hell's Kitchen. It was a stretch of city that reminded me of a grittier version of the Latin Quarter in Paris, both neighborhoods characterized by restaurant owners standing outside their doors, beckoning us to taste their food, everything from Turkish and Thai to Mexican and sushi. While cuisine definitely topped our list of New York "musts," we weren't there just for the food. We'd come to see Olivia and Ava sing Broadway favorites at Carnegie Hall. It was a trip we'd been planning for eight months.

What we hadn't planned was to make a local move that same calendar week. This included both selling and buying a house.

I suppose that's what happens when I choose the word "adventure" as my theme for a year. At its picking time, I seriously had idealistic visions of myself standing, much like Disney's Belle from *Beauty and the Beast*, in a field, singing about adventure . . . and then thoroughly enjoying whatever adventure came. The problem was that I'd ignored what immediately followed this song for Belle: a missing father, a creepy castle, a dungeon, and a beast. I'd forgotten that in all my favorite stories, adventure isn't simply an exciting, thrill-seeking activity that's cheer-worthy. Rather, adventures are sometimes "nasty disturbing uncomfortable things."[2]

Days before we boarded the plane to LaGuardia, we packed our belongings into a U-Haul and drove them eleven miles from one Georgia county to another. We traded our 3,357 square foot McMansion of four years for one about half the size. For us, it was a financial, as well as quality-of-life decision. We needed to pay off debt. But beyond that, we were ready to pour our time, money, and energy into experiences, rather than things like large home mortgages. It was a needed change. Yet that didn't necessarily make it an easy one.

> We technically had a home, but in our hearts we felt homeless.

As we stayed in that tenth-floor Manhattan hotel room and wandered the streets of Hell's Kitchen, neither of us longed for the familiar sights and sounds of home. Instead we grasped to figure out what home now felt like. Sure, our move had only involved eleven miles. Yes, we had the same jobs, the same church family, drove many of the same streets, and could still frequent our favorite haunts. We even had a lot of the same belongings that once fit nicely into our previous home, although now they crowded the attic and garage until we had the time and energy to purge. The problem was we hadn't lived in our new house long enough to miss it as "home." We technically *had* a home, but in our hearts we felt homeless.

The move had left us exhausted, stretched thin, and just plain uncomfortable. With our stress levels high and our hours of sleep low, we pondered if the risk we'd taken in uprooting ourselves from our "old normal" was worth this "new normal." It certainly didn't feel like it.

WHERE EVERYBODY KNOWS YOUR NAME

It all sounds a bit melodramatic, especially when you consider that this move was my seventh since marrying Ted and around my twenty-fifth since birth. The fact is, as I mentioned in the prologue, I'm no newbie to being uprooted. So, where's that toughness, that resilience I should have by now?

Honestly, I'm not sure.

What I do know is that this is the first move that's left me deeply contemplating, "What is home?"

It may seem like a dumb question to ask. Even so, for me it's been an important one to explore. If I can really understand what home is at its most profound level, then I can better comprehend why the loss of it can be so difficult. Maybe, like me, you've been asking yourself the same question. Perhaps you've recently said goodbye to your home too and can relate.

Here's what I've realized when it comes to defining home: I need to go beyond what an actual physical house is to how home makes me feel. I discovered in New York that what I grieved the most was not necessarily the house we'd left behind, as great as it was, but the emotions I associated with that house. It made me feel like I belonged, like I was supposed to be there in that house on that cul-de-sac in that neighborhood. It was familiar and comforting and welcoming. It was a place in which significant family memories had been created. Our new house didn't offer me that . . . yet.

> We aren't merely leaving behind a place, we're also giving up the sense of belonging we felt there.

I think this sense of belonging is what home is at its core. Writer and civil rights activist Maya Angelou put it well when she wrote, "The ache for home lives in all of us. The safe place where we can go as we are and not be questioned."[3] Home is a place that offers you and me emotional safety and inclusion. This is one reason saying goodbye to a home—whether it's trading one house for another locally, or trading an entire city for a different one—can cause us to feel as if we've lost something. The truth is, we have. We aren't merely leaving behind a place, we're also giving up the sense of belonging we felt there.

The grief you and I experience over losing home is something that takes time to process, and as I personally allow myself to do so, I find solace in knowing that I'm not the only one to ever grieve home. Others have walked through this before me.

A TALE OF TWO IMMIGRANTS

While in New York City, we visited Ellis Island. Located in Upper New York Bay near the Statue of Liberty, it was here that over twelve million immigrants entered the United States between 1892 and 1954. They traveled a lot farther than my eleven miles, and certainly couldn't bring enough belongings to fill any attics and garages. Each of these individuals bid farewell to their homes and made difficult journeys across oceans, fully knowing that they may never see some of their family and friends again. Unlike us, they didn't have technology like Skype or Facebook to easily and instantly reconnect with those they'd left behind. I imagine their grief at saying goodbye was deep and unbearable at times, comforted only by the hope they had of a better life on American shores.

As I think about the halls, dining rooms, and dormitories there, I'm reminded of two immigrants who left their homes centuries before Ellis Island was even established. While their goodbyes happened about a decade apart, like the immigrants who came to New York, these women also said farewell to the familiar and the comforting and the welcoming. Their names were Naomi and Ruth.

They lived sometime between 1400 BC and 1000 BC and their story's recorded in the Old Testament book of Ruth. It's a short read, consisting of only four chapters, yet for someone like me who's grieving the loss of a home, there's a lot I can learn from its leading ladies. Perhaps their historical narrative can encourage you too.

The story first sets its focus on Naomi, a wife and the mother of two sons. Due to a famine, she and her family leave their hometown of Bethlehem in Judah, or Israel as we call it now, and travel to the neighboring country of Moab, which today is modern-day Jordan. It's interesting to note that when the writer of Ruth describes this family's move in Ruth 1:1, he uses the word "sojourn." Sojourn means to "live temporarily,"[4] which tells me that Naomi and her family never planned to stay in Moab long. Yet only one verse later, we're informed that they "remained there" (Ruth 1:2). What started as a temporary exodus from home, turned into at least a decade.

If being forced to say goodbye to her home wasn't enough, it's during these ten years that Naomi faces more loss.

First, her husband, Elimelech, dies. Naomi is left a widow in a foreign land.

Second, her two sons, Mahlon and Chilion, decide to marry Moabite women named Ruth and Orpah. While Naomi grows to love her daughters-in-law, I imagine she was initially shocked and grieved by her sons' marital choices. Marrying a foreigner went against the Jewish teachings she'd been raised with and most likely passed on to her sons. Not only that, but these marriages also signified to Naomi that her sons had resigned to never return to Judah. Instead, they were putting down deep roots in Moab. Their sojourn into foreign territory had become permanent, which meant that as a widow dependent on them, hers had too.

This isn't the end of loss for Naomi, though. It isn't long before tragedy strikes again. It's somewhere around that ten-year mark that both Mahlon and Chilion die, leaving Ruth and Orpah widows, just like Naomi.

It's at this point that Naomi decides to return to Bethlehem after hearing that the famine is finally over. She attempts to persuade both

> We may not have a choice on whether we leave a much-loved home, but we do have a choice on how we'll respond to the grief we feel when it happens.

Ruth and Orpah to stay in Moab. Orpah agrees, but Ruth insists on going with Naomi. As Naomi had done a decade earlier, Ruth says goodbye to the only country she's known and becomes an immigrant.

What is it that I learn from these two women as I grieve the loss of my own home? The story of Ruth and Naomi offers some great lessons.

CHOOSE LOYALTY, NOT BITTERNESS

Over the years, I haven't always had a choice on whether I leave behind a much-loved home, but I have always had a choice on how I respond to the grief I feel when it happens. Ruth and Naomi each react to loss—which to be fair, also included the death of immediate family members—in drastically different ways. One woman chooses loyalty, while the other embraces bitterness.

Ruth devotes herself to Naomi and to Naomi's God. She determines that her love for her mother-in-law outweighs the comfort of remaining in the same, familiar place. And, once she does leave home and experiences the reality of saying goodbye, she doesn't falter. She's fervent in her loyalty. Ruth seeks out opportunities to take care of Naomi and provide for them both.

Naomi, on the other hand, becomes bitter. Quite literally. When she returns to Bethlehem, she tells her old friends and neighbors to no longer call her Naomi, which means "pleasant," but to call her Mara, meaning "bitter." Her reasoning? "For the Almighty has dealt very bitterly with me," she explains. "I went away full, and the LORD has brought me back empty. Why call me Naomi, when the LORD has testified against me and the Almighty has brought calamity upon me?" (Ruth 1:20–21). Naomi is so focused on her loss that it causes her to believe God only has pain planned for her.

It's easy for me to read Naomi's words and think, "I'd never respond to loss like that. I know that God's good and that He loves me." What I've found, though, is the more I believe God is intricately involved in all the details of my story, the more I'm tempted to do as Naomi did and go from "God is good" to "God is against me." I'm not proud of it, but there have been many times when it's exactly the way I've reacted.

How am I learning to combat this type of response?

I remind myself of what Scripture tells me. I feed myself and my ever-changing emotions the unchanging truth of God's Word. In Romans, I'm told:

> So what do you think? With God on our side like this, how can we lose? If God didn't hesitate to put everything on the line for us, embracing our condition and exposing himself to the worst by sending his own Son, is there anything else he wouldn't gladly and freely do for us? (Rom. 8:31 MSG)

This is just one of many passages in the Bible where I'm encouraged to believe that God is for me. Perhaps you're struggling to accept this in your current loss too. If so, I get it. I really do. I've experienced dark seasons permeated by one loss after another where everything seemed to indicate otherwise. If that's where you are, I encourage you to take some time, as I have, to write down verses that remind you of God's love for you. In those moments when you feel bitter over your loss, read them. If you aren't sure where to look for these, start by reading through the Psalms. Many of these songs—for example, Psalms 27 to 34—focus on how God tenderly cares for those who love Him when times are hard.

Cling to community, rather than send it away

As I mentioned, before Naomi returns to Bethlehem, she attempts to cut ties with Ruth and Orpah. To Naomi's credit, her attempt to send her daughters-in-law away is an unselfish gesture of love toward them. She encourages them to return to their families and hopefully marry again. She wants them to have happy and prosperous futures. At the same time, though, she seems to discount the importance of the emotional and familial ties she shares with them. After all, together these three women grieved the deaths of Mahlon and Chilion, which is no small thing. However, Naomi focuses solely on her inability to provide them with future husbands, and ignores their powerful bond of shared grief.

Ruth's reaction is to cling to Naomi. She doesn't concede to her mother-in-law's push for her to return to her parents and her former life. Instead, she holds tightly to the community she's currently in, telling Naomi, "Do not urge me to leave you or to return from following you. For where you go I will go, and where you lodge I will lodge. Your people shall be my people, and your God my God" (Ruth 1:16). Ruth is so resolute that Naomi gives up and allows her to come.

I'm slowly learning that there are people in my community who *want* to help.

There's a striking difference in how the two women engage community, isn't there? As I notice the distinctions between them, I realized that too often, once again, I'm more like Naomi than Ruth.

It's not that I push community away, as she does here, but I might as well. My problem is that I find it difficult to ask for help because I don't want to inconvenience anyone. I want to be the one *to* help, not the one who *needs* help. It's no biggie for me to change my plans to assist a friend, but I physically cringe at the thought of asking someone else to do the same for me.

I'm slowly learning, though, that there are people in my community who *want* to help. Just like me, they don't mind being inconvenienced. Most recently, it took a broken air conditioner to remind me of this.

A few days after we returned to Georgia from New York City, Ted left for Wisconsin to spend three weeks with his dad, who had been diagnosed with a brain tumor. His dad only had a short time left and we both agreed it was important for Ted to be by his side.

Shortly after Ted left, the air conditioner in our new-to-us house died. While a dead A/C unit is never a welcome plot twist, it's especially unpleasant in the middle of the summer in Georgia over a holiday weekend. We ended up waiting four days for a repairman.

When the repairman finally arrived, he proclaimed the culprit to be a dirty filter. We soon discovered the problem was more complicated than that, though, when two days later, the A/C went on strike a second time.

We weighed our options and determined our best course of action was to buy a new unit. The biggest issue, aside from the cost, was the timing. The fastest a new one could be installed was in three days.

The thought of several more days without air conditioning broke me. I packed the kids into the minivan, drove to the nearest home improvement store, and headed straight for the portable A/C aisle. With tears in my eyes and a tremble in my chin, I called Ted and told him I needed to make this three-hundred-dollar purchase. There was little he could say but, "Okay."

However, I was faced with yet another problem. The unit weighed almost seventy pounds. Once I arrived home with it, there was no way I could physically carry it into the house and set it up. Yet, as much as I needed help, I didn't want to inconvenience anyone.

Fortunately for me, the word "bother" isn't in Ted's vocabulary. He texted his men's breakfast group, asking for help.

Within an hour, one of our friends from church was at our house. He'd come straight from work to carry the unit in and set it up for me. Not only that, but he and his family extended an offer for us to stay at their house if ours remained too hot. Our community was ready and willing to help. First, though, we had to be brave enough to let them know we needed it.

This is only one example of how God is teaching me that community is important as I grieve the loss of home. It's the people, those who create meaningful experiences with us, that help us find that sense of belonging and safety for which we long. It's those friends who carry heavy air conditioners or offer to let us stay at their house who help a new place feel a little more like home. Their goodness helps ease the grief.

As the book of Ruth continues, Ruth and Naomi's bond strengthens, and God provides for the pair. Ruth goes on to marry a relative of Naomi's. Together, he and Ruth have a son named Obed. This son later becomes the grandfather of King David. It's this family line from which Jesus stems. While Ruth and Naomi didn't live long enough to see the Messiah born generations later as part of their family tree, you and I know this is how their story unfolds and we can marvel at it.

HOW TO FIND HOME

Unlike my most recent move, many of my moves haven't come with an already established community. Most of them have involved starting over in a new place from scratch. No family, no friends, no church home. It's possible that's where you find yourself right now. If so, I've come up with some strategies over the years to make a new place feel like home.

Remember the constants

Constants are those things that don't change. For me, the constant in all of my moves has been God. As a military wife, my friend Carlie Kercheval has found this to be true in her life too.

....

I remember it as if it were yesterday—the long journey home alone in January 2003 after dropping my husband off for boot camp in our home state of Washington. He and I wouldn't see each other again until after he completed his training and we both reached his first duty station in New York. As I drove away and left him standing there, tears were streaming down my face; my heart was pounding and my head was spinning as my lips attempted to form words and cry out to God.

The longing for home made a harsh entrance into my life shortly after this event. In the hours that followed, I came to realize that home was not a place—it was a calling. My calling to be home could only be fulfilled through God and His presence.

The next day the reality of my very first cross-country move from Washington to New York began to set in. I was overwhelmed to realize that the only community I had ever known would soon be 2,836 miles away. I was also still in shock that my husband would be going to war. The United States had recently invaded Iraq and we had learned that all new army recruits would be shipped off. In this time of transition, I came to know God and His love for us in a more intimate way.

The day our firstborn daughter and I flew from Washington to New York was one of the most emotionally exhausting days of my life. I said goodbye to everything: my entire family, my husband's family, our church family, my childhood friends, and our first home. We were leaving the only place I had ever known as home. That day I asked the Lord to show me how to handle this unsettling feeling. He answered me with this verse: "By wisdom a house is built, and through understanding it is established; through knowledge its rooms are filled with rare and beautiful treasures" (Prov. 24:3–4 NIV).

While I didn't fully understand what the Lord was showing me, a sense of peace came over me as I read these verses. I realized that the Lord had a plan for us in New York—one that would prove to be the foundation of the strong sense of home for which I longed.

The first Christmas in New York was really tough. We were so far from family; I spent most of the day in tears. At twenty-seven-years old, I had never spent a Christmas away from my mom or grand-ma. Yes, it was hard. However, the Lord kept reminding me of the verses in Proverbs 24, and my sweet husband prayed for me and held me close as we began to create our new "home" together.

With God's help I began slowly but surely working my way out into the communities on the military base. Before I knew it, we had made some great lifelong friends and found an amazing church community. We were thriving in our new home in New York.

In just two short months, we will be embarking on our eleventh move together. The whole New York experience has repeated itself over and over in our lives. Add in five separate yearlong deploy-ments and several months of training, and I can assure you that my life would have fallen apart if I didn't have a strong sense of home being rooted in Christ.

While moving never gets any easier from a logistical standpoint, it certainly has become easier from a spiritual standpoint. We've learned how to stay united through God's Word, prayer, and lots of healthy communication. We've learned to trust that God has gone before us and prepared the way for our exciting journey. We've learned that as long as we have God and one another, we are always home.

Without a doubt, home is not so much a physical place as much as it is a comfort in knowing God's plan is bigger than anything we can see. Now, as I prepare for yet another move, I am thankful that God will be with me every step of the way.

....

Remembering that God is my constant has been an important first step in making somewhere new feel like home, but it's not all I've learned to do with each move.

Let go of the place you left behind

I've also had to let go of the old in order to embrace the new. When I cling too tightly to what I've left behind, my attention is distracted from fully living in the present. I learned this the hard way.

When I was twenty, I moved with my parents from Southern California to Hilo on the Big Island of Hawaii. It wasn't a relocation I wanted to make because my affections for California ran deep.

So why did I move? After all, I *was* an adult and could have stayed behind.

A huge factor was finances. Even though I had a full-time job, I still lived with my parents and was slowly working toward a college degree. I didn't earn enough to live on my own in California *and* have money to pay school tuition out of pocket. Since my goal was to graduate from college without tens of thousands in loans, I opted to move to Hawaii, continue to live at home with my parents, and attend the state university there. Three years later, I earned my BA in Communication and graduated without any college debt. That's not to say I did it all with a good attitude. While I made the most of the communication and theater departments at my university, I never fully embraced where I was. I couldn't because I hadn't let go of from where I'd come. And because of that, I didn't enjoy Hawaii as much as I could or should have.

Carpe urbem (Seize your city!)

"Wow, you sure do get out!" one of my local friends commented. "In seven years, we haven't done as much as you have in seven months."

We'd recently moved from Springfield, Missouri, to Atlanta, Georgia. Since we arrived, my girls and I had explored at least half of the metro Atlanta area. While my out-and-about-ness with four kids may have seemed adventurous to some, by this point in my life, exploration had become the norm.

After moving as much as I had, I'd finally learned to *carpe urbem,* or in other words, "seize the city." I'd figured out ways to make the most of the places we lived. The older I'd gotten and the longer I reflected on my Hawaii experience, the more I determined I wanted to live with no regrets in the event that I had to face another moving van.

In what ways have I learned to seize my city?

First, I simply get out. I get out of the house. I get out of my comfort zone. And, once I *am* out, I don't keep to myself. Rather, I'm friendly and strike up conversations. I never know if the other person I decide to talk to at the park, library, bookstore, or zoo could become a close friend. It has happened.

Second, I explore the local culture. I've found social media is a great resource. Once I move to an area, I follow the social media pages of area attractions, whether it's the local history museum, library, or the performing arts center. This makes it easy for me to discover fun places of interest as well as free activities and events.

In John 10:10, Jesus says, "I came that they may have life and have it abundantly." I want to live an abundant life and maybe seizing my city, town, or rural neighborhood is one key to living life more abundantly. It's certainly one key to letting go of the place I've left behind and making a new place feel more like home.

With each move we've made, Ted and I have been purposeful about finding a church home.

Find a church home

During our weeping years, we moved from Colorado Springs to the Chicago suburbs. For us, it was a move of necessity. Ted needed a job and he found one near the Windy City. We brought with us more than a Penske truck stuffed full of earthly possessions, though. We also carried with us deep-seated grief over saying goodbye to a previous job and home. We arrived in Chicago wounded and limping. Our new church welcomed us in as family, bruises and all. They unconditionally loved on our kids, encouraged us in our marriage, and made us pot roasts when we needed them the most. Their kindness not only offered comfort to us in what felt like a hopeless season, but it also served to heal some of the hurt I'd felt years earlier after our painful small group experience.

With each move we've made, Ted and I have been purposeful about finding a church home. Sometimes, like Chicago, we're fortunate to discover the right fit for us quickly. Other times, it takes four or five or even six visits to different area churches. Once we do commit to a church, we aren't content to just show up on Sundays. We take the membership class and embrace the motto, "We have friends here; we just haven't met them yet." For us, diving into a church community helps make a new place feel like home faster.

Making and developing strong connections doesn't always happen instantly for us. The small group story I shared in chapter 2 is proof of that. Sometimes even when we do actively engage in a church community, it still takes time to make friends and we have experienced disappointment in the process. We're learning, though, not to give up if we don't immediately have that. We strive to be patient and continue to show up.

Five months after we stood in that hotel room on the tenth floor of a Manhattan Holiday Inn feeling homeless at heart, our family of six found ourselves back in Manhattan, this time renting a two-bedroom apartment in Hell's Kitchen for a month.

It turns out that the Carnegie Hall performance Ava did in June resulted in a second trip to New York City in July, this time to audition for the national tour of a Tony award–winning production. It was a second trip and an audition we couldn't have swung if we hadn't sold our house and lowered our monthly expenses.

"Adventure" continued to be our word for that year and into this current year too. Ava was cast as one of the seven children in the show. Saying yes to this new adventure has brought its own distinct joys and excitements, but it's also included discouraging challenges and has been uncomfortable on a regular basis.

Our family has spent the majority of the last eight months apart from one another, split between "home" and "the show on the road." As I write this, I'm sitting on a tour bus, traveling from Virginia to Tennessee. For most of this time, though, Ted has traveled from city to city with Ava, making many one-night only performance stops, while I've managed day-to-day life in Atlanta, solo parenting the other three kids. Along the way, we've had to learn how to stay connected via FaceTime, email, and short weekend meet-ups, and to give each other grace when we struggle to find time to communicate well.

There are days, sometimes weeks even, when saying goodbye to our last home still painfully haunts me, and it's been almost a year since the move. Some mornings when I'm at home and not on the road, I wake up, look around, and wonder if our new house will ever feel as familiar and comforting and welcoming as our previous one did. I even question if perhaps we made a mistake in moving.

Yet, this national tour has continued to challenge me to accept that home isn't necessarily a physical location where all of our family is all of the time. Instead, the transient nature of it has required that I daily view home as that sense of belonging we create and nurture with those we love. I'm learning by experience that it's a belonging our family can experience whether we were all safely within the walls of our Georgia house, in an apartment in New York City, or on the road at a hotel.

If like me, you're homesick at times too, it's my hope that God will gently meet you in your grief. May you too bravely attempt to trust that this story He is writing for you is one wrought with possibility and community, even when it feels lonely and far from it.

CHAPTER 4

JOBS

"Success consists of going from failure to failure without loss of enthusiasm."
— Winston Churchill[1]

Our fourth daughter Dorothy Jane's first glimpse of this world was filled with the sights and sounds of a hospital delivery room nestled in the chilly suburbs of Chicago; our home away from home that March evening in 2011.

Two days later, Ted was handed a pink slip. Talk about a metaphorical rain on our parade of newborn joy.

It was the second pink slip in less than a year. Only eight months earlier, there'd been cutbacks at the Colorado-based ministry where Ted had worked for several years. His role there ended and he reluctantly said goodbye. It happened not long after our miscarriage, in the midst of my battle with severe panic attacks, and as I struggled to trust God with a new, post-miscarriage pregnancy that would ultimately gift us with Dorothy.

In Chicago, we had hoped to escape the uncertain landscape of the unemployment we faced in Colorado and make a fresh start, but instead this second pink slip left us once again wading through its badlands, knee-deep in job loss muck. And there was something about *this* timing, *this* juncture in our lives that made it feel like a low blow as we slowly peeled ourselves off the ground after a knockdown. It had simply come *too* soon after that first pink slip, *too* soon into the panic attacks, and *too* soon after the miscarriage. Just when Dorothy's birth promised us joy, loss hit again. It felt like more than we could handle.

We blamed the losses on reduction in force, the economy, and even poor person-job fit. Yet regardless of the individual reasons behind each pink slip, all that really mattered was that in 2010 and 2011, employment odds weren't in our favor. Not even a little bit. We did our best to cling to our belief that God was good no matter what life hurled at us, but even so, our optimism and hope were in short supply.

Our energy, time, and devotion now stood divided between middle-of-the-night feedings and online job searches, first smiles and Women, Infants, and Children (WIC) applications, family bonding and the financial concerns of how to afford both rent on our Chicago townhome and a mortgage on our Colorado house that refused to sell. It was, just as author Jeff Manion describes in his book *The Land Between: Finding God in Difficult Transitions*, a "season of profound disorientation and chaos"[2] that left us "at a loss as to how to navigate the terrain."[3]

> **Disheartenment and disillusion can have a way of overshadowing expectation and possibility.**

These two consecutive job losses broke Ted. He was a man with two master's degrees, over twenty years of work experience, and a mad skill set. Throughout his career, he excelled at going above and beyond the demands given him and consistently put in extra hours. He was the picture of a dedicated team player . . . plus some. Yet now, he couldn't seem to hold a job. Did the qualities he prided himself on *really* matter? Were they still marketable?

They certainly hadn't marked him "safe" from reduction in force, the economy, or poor person-job fit. My once-confident husband felt like a loser.

HOPE FOR LOSERS

Of course, Ted's not the only one to have felt this way. Many of us have disappointments in our employment history, stretches of time when we've been unemployed or underemployed, and have felt the same emotions. Maybe you're feeling them now.

In the midst of unemployment, it's difficult, even seemingly impossible at times, to view job loss with hope. Disheartenment and disillusion have a way of overshadowing expectation and possibility. They did for us after that second pink slip. It was a fight to stay optimistic, one we struggled to win . . . but regularly lost. We grappled to fully and firmly believe that if God was indeed writing our story that our loss was a plot twist being penned with promise and not despair.

One of the things I learned when in graduate school studying film is what screenwriters label "rising action." It's at these points in the story—be it a film, television show, play, or book—when the hero is climbing uphill. These are the moments when things get complicated and hard, when loss seems imminent and success seems elusive. Here suspense introduces itself and tension mounts. Eventually this rising action results in a "climax" or "epiphany" when the protagonist reaches the top of a particular peak. It's a moment of greatest interest when there comes a wonderful turning point in the story. It could be that circumstances change, that situational breakthrough occurs. Many times, though, what changes is our hero. He or she grows in unexpected ways that are a direct result of the uphill struggle.

Job loss was part of our rising action. It was an arduous battle where we felt exhausted and defeated, yet had no choice but to keep climbing. In this difficult and discouraging process, we discovered a lot about our ideas of identity, confidence, and security and God's role in them. Here are a few things we learned.

God at work in identity

Many articles and books I've read encourage readers to resoundingly proclaim, "My identity is found solely in God and in nothing else." Identity is what makes us distinctly us and provides a sense of worth and value. While yes, it's foundational that our identities are firmly rooted in who God says we are, sometimes these type of statements can be misconstrued. For me, they can sway me to feel that my God-given identity doesn't include the work I do. As a result, I can feel guilty that how I define myself or even how Ted defines himself *is* influenced by the daily tasks accomplished and the "attaboys" received in return.

Here's the thing, though. When God made all of us, He designed us to find meaning and purpose in our earthly vocation. Whether we work a nine-to-five job at an office, telecommute, or are a stay-at-home mom, it's okay and good, even, that we find significance in work. Certainly Adam did when the Lord gave him the command to work the land and tend the garden.[4]

But for Ted and me, and maybe you too, a problem arises when we struggle to be balanced in our approach to work and identity. It's hard to find a healthy measure of satisfaction and value in our work, without letting it become the be-all and end-all of who we are. Ted and I both have to be careful in this area.

Because God made us to find value and meaning in our vocation, when a specific job or even career path ends—especially one that allows us to use well the talents, strengths, and skills with which God has gifted us—there's the potential to experience an identity crisis, or a questioning of our individual purpose and significance. We can despairingly contemplate whether we still matter now that our job has ended.

Ted certainly experienced this. He felt like a loser, in a capital L tattooed on his forehead sort of way. As he wrestled with his sense of worth, I watched and mourned this identity crisis. It was heart wrenching to witness my talented and devoted husband view himself with so little esteem.

My workaholic husband, and me to some extent too, were painfully learning that it's okay, albeit not at all fun, to be a loser from time to time. In our lives, past success had often driven us to find too much of our identity in work, to leave us unbalanced in where or in whom we found our value. Loss was helping us rediscover a better work-life balance. It sorely reminded us that, yes, God designed us to find a great deal of our meaning in work, but work alone shouldn't define us.

God at work in confidence

A few months after the second pink slip, Ted accepted a job in Missouri. It paid half of what he'd previously made—a beginner's salary, really—but we were desperate. We had four kids to feed and still hadn't sold our house in Colorado. Let's just say that financially, Charles Dickens would've labeled it the "worst of times."

For Ted, confidence-wise it wasn't much better. While the job in Missouri kept us from declaring bankruptcy, it did little to boost his waning self-esteem. Daily, he sensed that his out-of-the-box thinking was unwelcome, his twenty years of experience in web development unappreciated, and that the extra hours he willingly offered weren't valued as highly as punching the eight-to-five clock. He came home each night weary. We sometimes wondered why they hired him in the first place.

It was tempting at times to assume God was absent. There were days when it certainly felt like it. We had to constantly and consistently tell ourselves and each other that He hadn't left us to fend for ourselves in an unsatisfying position at a mediocre pay rate. As we did, we were also forced to reexamine where we'd placed our confidence.

At its simplest, confidence is defined in two ways. The first is as "a feeling of self-assurance arising from one's appreciation of one's own abilities or qualities."[5] This definition points to certainty or assurance in self, in what we can accomplish and provide by our own strength and skill. Much like constant success may drive us to invest too much of our identity in work, it may also encourage us to place too much reliance in our own competence and capabilities. The second is "the feeling or belief that one can rely on someone or something; firm trust."[6] This definition guides us away from ourselves and directs us toward someone or something outside of our own strength and skill. We're admonished to place our confidence in something greater than ourselves.

The two pink slips continually reminded us that no matter how hard Ted worked or how much we both wanted him to remain in a particular position, we couldn't compel an employer to keep him on staff. Likewise, we couldn't force a company to hire him. Where and when he worked weren't something we could magically arrange to meet all our financial and emotional needs. As much as we desired to be in control of how our story was being written, we weren't. Day by day and month by month, unemployment followed by this unhappy job gently pushed us to evaluate how much we actually trusted God. Slowly, it helped us develop a deeper confidence in Him even when uncertainty was our daily reality.

God at work in security

Unemployment didn't just affect our financial security. It also impacted the security, or freedom from worry, that we found in the comfort of routine and the normalcy of relational interactions.

Ted's regular routine changed drastically. No wake-up alarm was set. No shower immediately taken. No kisses to bid me goodbye and no drive to the office. Instead, he woke up on his own, remained in his pajamas, and spent the day at his computer, hunting for jobs online. Without his normal work routine, the structure he'd come to expect day-to-day vanished. His days began to blur together, dominated by screen time and the bloodshot eyes it produced. The lack of a predictable, productive routine left Ted grumpy and depressed. Antidepressants and "mood-improving" lamps became part of our routine.

What I didn't expect was how unemployment altered the normalcy of our relationships. While Ted and I managed to keep our connection strong, it brought an awkwardness and strain to interactions with former coworkers who attended the same church we did. It became the sole focus of our phone conversations with family. We grew tired of talking about job loss and being told what we needed to do to change Ted's employment status and fix our finances.

Many of the familiar aspects of our everyday lives that had once made us feel secure were now gone or acutely changed. It was difficult and jarring. This shakeup of everything that made us feel secure uncomfortably pushed us to remember that our true freedom from care, anxiety, or doubt could only come from God.

> **We have to purposely determine where to fix our focus—either on our changing circumstances or on our unchanging God.**

I won't lie, it wasn't easy. Unemployment invoked a myriad of emotions such as anger, frustration, fear, and depression. And, Ted and I didn't often feel the exact same emotions at the exact same time. In the midst of this, it was often difficult to remember truth and to believe that God was for us, rather than against us. Every single day, we had to purposely determine where to fix our focus— either on our changing circumstances or on our unchanging God.

TODAY'S RESPONSE TO LOSS SHAPES TOMORROW'S YOU

I've shared a lot about job loss as the wife of someone who's been unemployed. But do I have firsthand experience with it? Do I know what it's like to actually lose a job?

I do.

As I write this, it's only been a few months since my role as managing editor for a high profile website ended after almost four years. The website changed company hands and with that came a new vision, a new team, and new demands.

Saying goodbye to this role has compelled me to ask myself hard questions in regard to my identity, confidence, and security. I've found myself revisiting lessons learned in Ted's unemployment and also encouraging myself that God has a purpose in adding an end date for this position on my resume, even if I don't know what it is yet.

Most importantly, though, I've been cautioning myself to tread carefully in how I respond to this job loss. For Ted and me, God has worked in and through past unemployment to coax us toward the kind of people He intends us to become. My attitude and perspective, though, always directly affects whether the character development I experience is positive or negative. In short, today's response to loss shapes tomorrow's me.

I also see this in the lives of two of Jesus' close friends, men whose reactions to loss took them to diametrically opposed results. The outcome of their lives vividly illustrates for you and me that how we react in the present really does affect who we become in the future.

THE LASTING LEGACIES OF JUDAS AND PETER

When you read the name "Judas Iscariot," what descriptive words immediately come to mind? Maybe for you it's "betrayer," "traitor," or even "backstabber."

If, by chance, you're unfamiliar with Judas and his story, he was one of Jesus' twelve disciples and served as the group's treasurer. He's the most infamous member of the Savior's inner circle of friends, remembered best for betraying Jesus with a kiss.

Here's what's interesting, though. Jesus had *two* disciples who betrayed Him. Judas wasn't the only one.

There was also Peter. After Jesus' arrest, this friend flat out denied that he even knew Jesus. I'd call that betrayal. After all, to betray is "to hurt (someone who trusts you, such as a friend or relative) by not giving help or by doing something morally wrong."[7]

Here's the thing: Because of the contrasting ways these two men reacted to their betrayals, I remember them differently. Perhaps you do too. I think of Peter as a pillar of the early church, while I remember Judas as a traitor and a coward. In fact, when I searched the word "betray" in an online thesaurus, a synonym for it was "Judas kiss."[8] His villainous legacy is *that* well ingrained in our cultural understanding of the man.

How did Judas's and Peter's drastically different reactions following their pivotal moral collapses determine their long-lasting legacies? Let's look back at their stories.

Shortly before Jesus is arrested, tried, and crucified, He sits down to eat dinner with His disciples. Among them are both Judas and Peter. At this point, Judas has already made a covert deal with the chief priests and the officers of the temple guard. He's taken thirty coins in exchange for handing Jesus over to them away from the crowds. All he needs to do now is make good on his promise.

What's interesting is that during dinner, Jesus doesn't avoid the topic of betrayal. He doesn't pretend like He's clueless. Rather, He brings it up more than once, which leads His dozen friends to question, "Is it me?" It isn't long before Jesus identifies Judas as the betrayer and exhorts him, "Hurry and do what you're going to do" (John 13:27 NLT).

Jesus then attempts to explain to His friends that He's going to be arrested and that they'll all abandon Him when He is. Impulsive and outspoken Peter can't help but protest. He confidently proclaims, "Even if everyone else falls to pieces on account of you, I won't" (Matt. 26:33 MSG). He boldly asserts, "I will lay down my life for you" (John 13:37).

Jesus isn't flattered by Peter's expression of devotion, though. He doesn't thank him for declaring to unconditionally stand by His side. Instead, He responds with this: "Before the rooster crows tomorrow morning, you will deny three times that you even know me" (John 13:38 NLT).

Ouch.

Understandably, Peter seems either hurt or insulted. Unfortunately, the New Testament writers don't record the tone of his response, or the emotion that fuels it, so it's not absolutely clear which one. But we do know that Peter rebuts. He declares, "Even if I have to die with you, I will never deny you!" (Matt. 26:35 NLT).

Unfortunately, denial is in Peter's future. Only hours later, Peter is asked three times by three different people if he's one of Jesus' friends. Each time, fear becomes his master and he utters phrases such as "I do not know the man" (Matt. 26:74). And, just as Jesus had predicted, a rooster crows an ironic amen to Peter's denials.

Here are two men who both betrayed Jesus. Two men who were within His inner circle and, in a sense, employed by Him. Here's where the actions they take in reaction to loss determine how they are remembered today.

They let their emotions drive their actions differently

Both Judas and Peter failed at their jobs. It's true that their actions of betrayal aren't equivalent in measure. Peter insisted to servant girls that he didn't know Jesus and used expletives to accentuate his point, but that's not as severe as Judas selling out Jesus to be publicly executed. There's a clear difference in the extremity of their duplicity. But if examined at a more basic, simple level, it's accurate to say each of these men lets Jesus down.

Just as they both failed at their jobs, they also both experienced remorse. They regretted their decisions and their deeds. Peter wept bitterly after the rooster crowed, while Judas returned the money he'd been paid. Yet after these initial actions signifying remorse, they allowed their feelings of anguish to develop and drive their post-betrayal actions differently.

Peter responded with *conviction*. When I look that word up in the dictionary, I find a definition along the lines of "to impress with a sense of guilt."[9] However, in Scripture the word conviction means to feel godly sorrow, a sense of heartbreak that leads us to repentance.[10] I see this with Peter. His remorse leads him to repent, to "turn around" from his poor actions. His conviction drives him to seek forgiveness and restoration. As a result, after the resurrection, Peter's relationship with Jesus is strengthened and his faith increased.

Judas, on the other hand, experienced *condemnation*. While conviction ultimately built Peter up, condemnation tore Judas down. He was acutely aware of his failure and he allowed his remorse to drive him to take his life rather than pursue mercy and reconciliation. Judas didn't understand that his betrayal of Jesus didn't have to be the end of his story; it didn't have to be that for which he's best remembered.

Imagine what would have happened if Judas had responded differently to the remorse he felt. What if instead of measuring himself by his betrayal, he had stepped back and viewed his life as a whole, humbled by the fact that three years earlier Jesus had chosen him? There had only been twelve brought into the Savior's inner circle and he was one of them. Judas failed to view the totality of his life and, as a result, we remember him for his worst act on his worst day.

They made different decisions in regard to community

Three days after he denied his friendship with Jesus, Peter was still with the other disciples. Despite his momentary unfaithfulness, he remained in his trusted community. Peter didn't isolate himself from his friends and hide in shame and fear. Instead, he stayed in the group.[11]

Unlike Peter, Judas separated himself from community. We have no recorded account of him seeking out the other disciples. Even though he returned the money, telling the chief priests and elders, "I have sinned by betraying innocent blood" (Matt. 27:4), Judas failed to repent in the presence of the men with whom he'd spent three years ministering.

> As you grieve job loss, it's important to not isolate yourself from others.

Those whom, outside of Jesus Himself, Judas's actions hurt the most. Judas allowed his behavior to drive him to isolation and ultimately to suicide.

The difference between how Peter and Judas engaged community reminds me that as I grieve job loss, it's important to not isolate myself from others. This doesn't mean I need to divulge how I'm feeling or the challenges I'm facing to everyone who asks. That's emotionally draining and solicits a lot of unwanted advice. What it does mean is that, as Peter did, I continue to surround myself with trusted individuals who not only encourage me when I struggle, but who rally to help me through it.

But, as Ted and I have found, sometimes remaining in community is a struggle. It isn't always easy. As hard as our friends and family attempt to support us, there are instances when they simply don't understand what we need in a particular season of loss. As a result, there are moments when interactions with them feel frustrating, rather than encouraging. It could be that you're experiencing this right now. If so, there are a few things we're learning to put into practice to improve this.

Be specific about what we don't need

A natural default for many people is to see a problem and want to fix it. Let's face it, it's easier to offer practical steps on how to change a situation than to simply sit and feel the grief of it. Yet when we've been in sorrow, we often find quick-fix solutions disheartening. We know that our situation isn't that simple. If it were, we'd have already changed our circumstances.

Not only that, but many times those who offer us suggestions don't know or understand all the details of our individual circumstances. Also, they may not take our unique personalities into account and how our temperaments influence our reaction to loss. So rather than giving us advice informed by these factors, we're presented with what *they* would want in the situation. The problem is it may not be what we need. This is why sometimes it's helpful to be direct and specific about what we don't need.

When my friend Megan's part-time position of twelve years was eliminated due to budget cuts and other changes in the ministry for which she worked, she sadly said goodbye to her dream job. "I loved the people I worked with and the ministry aspect of the job as well," she shares. "The work I was doing was fulfilling, gave me the opportunity to experience and try all kinds of new things, and was something I truly loved being a part of."

Following the loss, Megan faced the difficult task of telling others. "My personality type includes descriptors like 'introvert' and 'internal processor,'" she notes. "So when I was let go, my first inclination was to hide. In fact, I think I texted my mom and sisters something along the lines of, 'Wanted you to know my job has been eliminated and I don't really want to talk about it.'" Megan's family was quick to understand. "I am super thankful they respected that request," she says, "and let me bring it up again with them in my own time."

As we seek to clarify our needs, it's important to, as Megan did, exercise gentleness in our words. In Colossians 4:6, Paul instructs, "Let your speech always be gracious." When we're frustrated and grieving, sometimes it's more difficult to accomplish this. An easy way to make sure we do is to use what's called a "communication sandwich."

A communication sandwich is the practice of using praise and affirmation to sandwich criticism, much like you might place liverwurst between two slices of freshly baked rye bread. Here's an example of what it might sound like when related to job loss:

Praise/Affirmation

"I'm so grateful for your care and support as I grieve the loss of my job. It means a lot to me to know you are here for me and that you understand what it's like."

Criticism

"I know that all your words of advice come from a place of love and experience. Right now, though, I'm not ready for ideas on what I should do with my finances or where I should seek out a new job. I think I will be ready soon, but for now I need to make sense of this loss."

Praise/Affirmation

"Like I said, I am thankful for you and your encouragement right now. Your love and support mean so much to me!"

While the communication sandwich doesn't work with everyone, in general, I've found that it's not as difficult for others to swallow our constructive criticism when they know that we also recognize and appreciate what they're doing well. A communication sandwich allows us to share what we'd like to see changed in a way that accomplishes exactly that.

Be specific about what we do need

Other people can't read my mind. So I don't just tell them what I *don't* need, I help them know what I *do* need. They're willing to be there for me, they just need direction.

One way to do this is to work it into my communication sandwich. In the criticism section, I might add: "As I navigate this new season of loss, I'd love it if you were available to just sit with me and listen to how I'm feeling. I really need someone to be willing to cry and pray with me."

A second way is to simply be direct. If I'm asked, "What can I do? Do you need anything?" I try not to be afraid to answer yes and be specific. I have had friends tell me, "I need baby formula when you're at Costco. Could you pick that up for me?" I was happy to do so. It can be scary to flat out state the needs I have and how someone can help fill them, but it doesn't hurt to ask. The worst they can say is no.

Megan remembers well what she needed most. "The first month contained many tears, especially when I did broach the subject with friends and family or they broached it with me." She says, "I didn't tell a lot of people what was going on, but I did tell family and close friends so they could be praying."

Communicating what we do and do not need are two helpful ways Ted and I strengthen our support system during job loss, but what if we aren't the ones who are unemployed? How do we strive to support someone else, and what can you do for those in your life facing unemployment?

WHAT AN UNEMPLOYED LOVED ONE NEEDS MOST

If you and I are walking through someone else's job loss with them, the most important gift we can offer them is our ears. We can actively practice what James advises in James 1:19, which is "be quick to listen, slow to speak."

Many of us have a personal story of job loss, which can sometimes lead us to believe we are an expert on unemployment. The truth of the matter is: we *are* an expert on our own situation and what it feels like, but we *aren't* an authority on someone else's.

Our eagerness to offer advice may be well-intended, but many times if it isn't specifically asked for, it can be ill-timed and unhelpful. This doesn't mean we can't say anything at all. "I'm so sorry" or even "I don't know what to say" are helpful. These are words our loved one *does* need to hear because they acknowledge loss and validate grief. But, when it comes to our words of wisdom, the best initial action to take is to willingly listen and hold back our advice unless it's solicited. Megan shares how grateful she was for these type of people. "I am thankful for those who listened patiently," she says, "when I did eventually dump what I had been processing on them. I am also thankful for those who were sounding boards without offering a lot of unsolicited advice."

When we actively listen, we're also less likely to push others to grieve too quickly. We're less inclined to encourage them to take actions for which they aren't emotionally equipped yet. Megan notes that one of the things she hasn't been ready to do is see her former coworkers in person. "While I sought out community and shared this loss with family and close friends, reaching out to the community I worked with has been harder. I have not been back to the office or seen people face-to-face yet. I'm just not ready for that and I think that is okay." Part of listening well is taking note of areas, such as this one, where our loved one may need more time to process and then lovingly allowing them the time to do so.

JOB LOSS "AFTERMATH"

Due to my recent job loss, our finances are tighter than they were a few months ago. Yet, as I paid for groceries this week, it struck me that even still, I'm able to shop without the assistance of WIC. We couldn't do this for the first year of Dorothy's life.

Her early days were those of matching gallons of milk, cans of beans, and the correct ounces of cheese to WIC checks. Those were the shopping trips where I swallowed my pride as I organized items according to voucher at the checkout line for all to see. I look back and I'm thankful the help was available to us. I'm grateful for every sip of milk, spoonful of beans, and bite of cheese we were given.

Dorothy recently celebrated another birthday. For us, another year has passed since that second pink slip brought us WIC checks. While Ted now has a steady job, I haven't forgotten how hard those days were. Unemployment broke us and transformed us in ways we never anticipated or ever desired.

The truth is, sometimes I still fear facing them again, simply because I know how fragile the job market and economy can be. There are nights when I lie awake at four a.m. worrying about Ted's position or the work I have, about bills and medical insurance, and about what we'd do if the status of our stability unexpectedly changed. What I learned during past unemployment didn't "cure" me of all job-related anxiety. What it did do, though, was make me more aware of my constant need to remind myself that God is writing a good story for me and my family; one penned with promise and not despair, whether it feels like it or not.

If the loss you're mourning is one of unemployment, it's my prayer that in the midst of your own uphill climb, one most likely filled with fear, uncertainty, and disheartenment, that you too will continually seek to put your trust in a loving God who is for you. It may be extremely difficult at times to believe that He is still at work when you're not, but it's my hope that you will bravely choose to believe that He is.

CHAPTER 5

....

DREAMS

"Nothing that grieves us can be called little."
— Mark Twain[1]

When I was six, I wanted to be a schoolteacher. Now over thirty years later, I *am* a teacher, but not the kind I once imagined.

Yes, I specialize in phonics, history, and even math. Well, as long as the math stays elementary and doesn't venture into algebra. When the x's and y's start appearing regularly, that's when I call in outside help. Yet instead of leaving the house five days a week and teaching twenty or more students, I instruct our four daughters at home, 99 percent of the time in my pajamas. And, if we're going for full disclosure here, instruction happens *after* I drink a cup of coffee or two, but *before* I brush my hair or teeth. Priorities, right?

If you haven't already guessed, I'm a homeschool mom.

Some days everything clicks and lessons go smoothly. No one cries or tattles or decides that directions on worksheets are optional or should be completed with invisible ink. It's Instagram tidy and Facebook pretty.

Other days, when the tears flow—both from the kids *and* from me—I admit that I feel a tinge of envy for the moms whose school-aged children boarded the big yellow bus that morning. The ones whose daily battles differ from mine. On those days, I have to remind myself that for *our* family, this is the right decision.

Even though I now bear the title "teacher," I didn't carry this dream from age six until age thirty-one, when Olivia became school ready.

Once I hit my teens, the allure of teaching wore off. Instead, I was newly intrigued with the magic and influence of television producing. At around fourteen, it was decided. I was trading in aspirations of chalkboards for clapboards, lesson plans for scripts, and teacher break rooms for craft services. This decision went on to direct my educational plans right up through graduate school. I graduated with a master's degree in communication with a focus in cinema-television producing. I even promised my prospectus committee that someday I *really* would pitch the script I'd written a business plan for as my final project.

I never did . . . pitch it, that is. Something happened that I didn't anticipate at fourteen. Or at eighteen. Not even at twenty-two. I met a crazy-haired, piano-playing, website-designing man named Ted toward the end of my first semester of grad school who changed all my previous determinations about marriage.

Unlike my Grandma Schmidt who attended college with the intent of majoring in the pursuit of a husband, I didn't arrive at grad school with any intention of marrying. Marriage wasn't on my immediate radar. Yet a little over a year after Ted and I first met, my independent, bent-on-a-career-first, maybe-a-family-later self got married. Eight months after we said "I do" and five months before I finished my master's program, two very faint lines on a pharmacy-bought pregnancy test announced that I was to be a mom.

I sensed God calling me to lay down my dream.

Now, with a new husband and a baby on the way, my dream of being a television producer wasn't so easy. It didn't just involve me anymore. I knew that, if pursued, my career could mean eighty- to ninety-hour work weeks, perhaps even regular travel. It wasn't exactly conducive with the amount of time I personally wanted to spend with Ted and our soon-to-be-oxygen-breathing daughter.

And that's when it happened. I sensed God calling me to lay down my dream. The one I'd planned for and nurtured for over a decade.

I realize that in sharing my story of how I became a homeschool mom, I need to tread carefully. For some of you, perhaps there's a temptation to interpret my choices as something I view as prescriptive—formulaic, even—for all women. And that's frustrating because your story is quite different from mine. Please know, that's not my intention at all.

The decisions I made were deeply personal, and the right ones specifically for me. I know, love, and deeply respect other women whom God has called to do something entirely different with their lives. For many of them, this includes pursing the career aspirations He birthed within them and seeing these dreams realized.

There's my childhood friend who is a physician and a mother. She's using her education and training to help heal people, while also loving on a husband and two children. There's my friend from grad school who is fulfilling her dream of screenwriting and also raising two little boys. This amazingly talented writer is able to balance both. And then there's my friend who has dreamed for years of ministering overseas in the Middle East. Recently, God fulfilled that longing for her and her family.

Each of these women cause me to marvel at the God who writes unique stories for unique individuals. Our tales and our callings aren't the same, and that's a good thing. Our communities are richer because of it.

Some of you, though, do know what it's like to say goodbye to a sought-after career choice. And for you, this story—*my* story—hits deep and hard.

UNLIKE FATHER ABRAHAM

At first, the decision to lay down this dream felt easy. It seemed that letting go of it wasn't as hard as I first anticipated.

Looking back, I attribute it to the pregnancy hormones, that God-ordained regimen of HGC, progesterone, estrogen, Relaxin, and oxytocin that I was on. The divine elixir that helps grow and protect a new life for nine months *in utero*. Once I got past the constant nausea and less-than-healthy Big Mac cravings, its influence left me so preoccupied with tiny clothes, baby registries, and birth plans that I didn't have the time or need to think of previous aspirations.

What I didn't realize at the time is that I'd never grieved the loss of my dream, and I should have. With grieving often comes closure, and I didn't have that. While the excitement of motherhood temporarily overshadowed any feelings of sorrow, it was only a matter of time before they surfaced and I had to come to terms with the fact that life in my mid-to-late twenties wasn't what I'd expected it to look like back when I was fourteen, or eighteen, or even twenty-two.

It wasn't until after Olivia was born and then Ava eighteen months later, that the grief finally hit me, mostly in waves.

I'd be at home, breastfeeding every couple hours, and watching reruns of the early seasons of *Gilmore Girls* when it would happen. I'd remember someone I knew who'd toured Warner Bros. Studios in Burbank and had been given the opportunity to walk the streets of the fictional Connecticut town of Stars Hallow. With the memory, would come what author Robin Jones Gunn calls a "quiet sadness"[2] because working on a studio lot had been *my* dream.

Or the mail would bring the latest edition of the alumni magazine from my grad school. It often praised the accomplishments of female graduates who'd gone on to pursue and excel in their chosen fields and professions. Law, politics, and, yes, even filmmaking. Sure, these women were rightly praised. Just like me, they were being faithful to chase after what God was personally calling them to do. Yet even so, I couldn't help but notice that the stories of women with degrees who had chosen to stay home and raise their kids were sorely missing. In my fragile, exhausted state of being a mommy to two kids under the age of two, I felt left out. Forgotten, even.

While I didn't regret my decisions, honestly there were moments when I did wish that the laying down of my dream was more like Abraham's laying down of Isaac so long ago on a mountain in Moriah. You know, the Old Testament story where God provided another way: a ram in place of a boy. Where He saw fit to simply test Abraham, and not actually let him sacrifice this long-awaited fulfillment of a dream.

But it wasn't. And it still isn't.

Unlike Abraham, God hasn't handed this dream back to me after I proved I was willing to give it up. Instead, He's slowly showed me that His plan is different from what I'd originally believed it to be. With time, I've come to see that, perhaps, my dream wasn't ever really a means to a specific field, but instead a way to get me in the right place at the right time to meet that crazy-haired man of mine, birth babies, and eventually pick up the pen to use narrative in a different way.

WHEN REAL LIFE DOESN'T MATCH OUR IDEAL

My friend Salina knows well what it is to see God bring change through intense disappointment and the loss of a dream. When her son, Salem, was diagnosed with autism, she found herself deeply grieving what had been her firmly held hope for an autism-free life.

My journey with autism began before I had kids. When Salem was still in utero, we labored over everything from breastfeeding to vaccines because autism was my greatest fear. I consulted doctors and naturopaths. I read books. Bottom line: If I could help it, my kid was not going to get autism.

Autism spectrum disorder is so mysterious—so confusing and multifaceted. No glaring physical evidence, which means he would more often be judged and misunderstood. And then there is the fear of not being able to connect with my child. Wave upon wave of grief just at the thought.

After Salem was diagnosed, I found myself on my own spectrum ranging from hatred to despair. I hated autism from the onset. I said at least once a day, "I love my son. But I hate autism." Or, "I didn't sign up for this." And then what's worse is I hated my friends and relatives with neurotypical kids. I burned and seethed and cursed and ran. Literally, I ran twenty miles a week because it was the only time I could cry without little people watching.

Then despair set in over the emotional, physical, and financial uncertainty of *our entire life*. It was all too much. My husband, Clark, pulled me aside at a family reunion after I sneered at his cousin and her irritatingly "normal" toddler and said, "If you don't surrender this, you are going to unintentionally make a bad situation worse." So, I backed away from hatred, came home, and checked myself into therapy.

My counselor asked me the hard questions. She acknowledged that autism is a *big* deal, but she reminded me that it isn't the *only* deal I'm working on. I have a marriage, a ministry, interests, etc., and we needed to somehow compartmentalize this. She asked me to picture my life twenty years from now. What kind of marriage did I hope to have? What sort of quality of life did I hope to provide for my other children? She encouraged me to put together a twenty-year "survival" plan. This included getting immediate help by way of respite workers, babysitters, and people besides me that knew my son and loved our family and could provide a strength that I was certainly lacking.

She cautioned me from turning Salem's autism into an all-consuming driving force in our family and offering my marriage and my other children on the altar of his recovery. The reality is that I could enlist every therapy track under the sun and his quality of life may only be just so good. It was at that point that I resisted punching her in the face and just settled for taking her advice instead. I had enough relational change in the bank with this counselor that I knew her counsel was wise.

First fear, then hatred, then despair, and finally acceptance (sort of) . . .

I started listening to Mark Driscoll's sermons on my long runs. Probably because he screams a lot and I felt like screaming all the time. He challenged me to "suffer until I'm grateful for it. Then and only then the suffering will not go to waste." I came home and told Clark I still had so far to go because I couldn't *ever* fathom being grateful for autism. And yet, with Salem's autism has come a divinely tailored blend of supernatural *and* natural provision—relationships and resources that on my best game I could never have whipped up for him otherwise. I am convinced there is a special grace reserved for families with autism. A few perks:

1. Autism *cured* me of comparing my kids' development to other children because the "typical" rules don't apply. (Also, it cured me of getting embarrassed by my child's behavior in public. Again, we're following another game strategy here.)
2. I am nowhere *near* as critical or judgmental of other families. I have been able to cry with mothers in the school parking lot who are at their wits' end over their child's behavior and development, and when I say, "I get it," I really do get it.
3. It has expanded my personal ministry. Families with special needs are about the most hopeless group of walking dead I've ever seen. I go to these community meetings sometimes, or even just sit in the doctor's waiting room and look into these parents' eyes. It's as if the lights went out some time ago and they are just waiting out their prison sentence. Hope is needed there desperately.

4. I'm actually coming to appreciate the fact that Salem is mostly "oblivious" to the people around him. He has his people he prefers, but when I look at and listen to the kids his age and what they talk about and the humor they use and all the "garbage out," I am more and more thankful that Salem doesn't copy them and that most of the time he's completely untouched by their influence. This, I think, can serve him well.

5. We know what victory is when Salem spontaneously shows affection, or compassion, or humor (in his own subtle way), or when he joins his Sunday school class during the worship time instead of running into the church hallway screaming and covering his ears like he did nine months ago. It makes our world.

6. Above all, I'm so grateful that God corrected me this early in my motherhood journey from believing that I was the Master of My Child's Fate. Coming to grips with that was and has been incredibly liberating.

....

While my unfulfilled dream is markedly different from Salina's, I too learned a hard, but liberating truth as I grieved. It beckons back to job loss and identity. I realized that I'd put too much emphasis on my worth being tied directly to my aspirations and the fulfillment of them. I'd strongly believed that if I were impacting culture with television shows my life would have greater value than it did at home changing diapers and filling up sippy cups with strawberry milk. I came to see that I was wrong. God had specifically called me to love and serve my husband and kids, and because of that, there wasn't anything more "valuable" that I could personally be doing. It was a quieter route than I'd originally hoped, but no less important.

HOW TO STOP FEAR FROM ROBBING YOU OF COMMUNITY

I wish I could tell you that my grieving process was short. That once those waves of sorrow first hit, that I was able to work through them quickly. But I wasn't. It took me several years. And, the truth is, sometimes I still feel a tinge of that quiet sadness. I suppose that's expected considering I live in Georgia, a state where the local film and television industry is booming.

But the difference between then and now is that I talk openly, both privately and publicly, about the surrendering of my dream. Back then, I didn't. Instead of inviting Ted and close, trusted friends into the depths of my grief, I allowed fear to keep me from vulnerably and unashamedly grieving within the safety of my community.

> **I can only move forward and do better when faced with future disappointments.**

It's unfortunate that I can't go back to my former self and offer the wisdom that I've learned in the interim. Then perhaps, my grieving process wouldn't have been so lonely. But I can only move forward and do better when faced with future disappointments.

Although I can't encourage the past me, maybe you're in a place that's similar to where I was. Maybe you're struggling to reach out to those around you and be vulnerable. If so, there are some things I wish I'd done differently that I hope you might find helpful.

Refuse isolation

At the time, I didn't realize that in internalizing my grief, I was also isolating myself. Not only from friends, but also from my husband. In some ways, I was being like Rick from Casablanca—a relational refugee.

It's true that Ted was an "insider" to my grief. He was privy to my decision not to pursue the career I'd worked so hard toward. The problem was, when the grief finally hit three years and two babies into our marriage, I feared if I were *too* open and *too* honest that he'd interpret my feelings as discontentment, that he'd read them as complaints and resentment. The thought of being 100 percent transparent about it with him brought with it the fear of misunderstanding and unintentional wounds. I loved Ted deeply and I didn't want anything, including my delayed grief, to negatively affect our relationship.

When it comes to the loss of your dream, it could be that you're doing the same. Rather than share your feelings with those closest to you—whether a husband, a family member, or a close friend— you keep them buried inside. Your motivation may be different from mine, but your actions are similar. If this is you, make the decision, as scary as it may feel, to refuse isolation and determine not to cut off this part of yourself from others.

Instead, take action. Start small. Think of one person you feel comfortable enough to open up to, someone with whom you already have a strong relationship and who sets you at ease. Then schedule a specific time to talk and be committed to showing up.

> When it came to my friends, I didn't fear unintentional wounds, but I did fear misunderstanding . . . and judgment, even.

Share fear

Courage is "grace under pressure,"[3] Ernest Hemmingway once penned. What did he mean by this? The writer of a *New York Times* article explains that for Hemmingway, "the test for his characters, as for himself, was the ability to face defeat without panic."[4] He notes that in his best works, Hemmingway wrote about "life at the edge, men and women up against the wall, desperate situations rendered through fables of violence and defeat."[5] People who were brave even when fear and failure beckoned them not to be.

So while the dictionary may define "bravery" or "courage" as "the quality of mind or spirit that enables a person to face difficulty, danger, pain, etc., *without* fear,"[6] I find Hemingway's words more accurate. Most often, true courage requires that we face what frightens us even when we *are* still afraid.

This isn't easy though. It certainly wasn't—and at times, still isn't —for me.

When it came to sharing the grief I experienced over my career aspirations, fear didn't merely keep me from opening up to Ted. It also hindered me from opening up about my struggle with other women. Fear kept me from freely and vulnerably talking about the loss in the nursing mother rooms at our local church or on playdates at parks with other moms. It left me censoring myself at coffee shops over lattes and hot chocolate. I allowed it to prevent me from confiding in friends who may have been able to come alongside me and say, "Me too."

When it came to my friends, I didn't fear unintentional wounds, but I did fear misunderstanding . . . and judgment, even. Would I be considered silly and ungrateful and privileged for feeling sorrow over a lost dream when my life was so full and when I had so much? Would the honest sharing of my feelings be stifled by correction, rather than met with empathy? The longer I harbored and fed those fears, the longer I didn't share and the longer I isolated myself. Because of this, I missed out on community.

I challenge you to learn from my mistakes, to realize that fear doesn't need to hold you back. You don't have to be rid of it to reach out. I love what Matt Damon's character in the film *We Bought a Zoo* says. He states, "Sometimes all you need is twenty seconds of insane courage. Just literally twenty seconds of just embarrassing bravery. And I promise you, something great will come of it."[7]

When it comes to your loss, have twenty seconds of insane courage and use it to confide in that one person you've identified. I think you'll find that when you do, fear will start to lose its power.

Use loss to encourage others

It was several years later, after the birth of Savannah, that I remember finally talking openly about the grief. First publicly in articles, and then privately with friends. It may have been a backward way of doing it, but for me there was a safety in being vulnerable behind my keyboard that didn't come so easily face-to-face.

I quickly discovered I wasn't alone. Others began to share their stories of crumbled dreams with me and I found that most of us, if we're honest, feel sadness over some hope never realized or an expectation left unfulfilled.

For many, it hasn't been career related like mine. Some I know have mourned the reality that marriage didn't happen by their ideal age, and still hasn't happened yet. They continue to wait, intimately acquainted with the words of Proverbs 13:12 that "hope deferred makes the heart sick." I've listened as others have grieved each pregnancy test coming back negative, each month when their longing for a baby remains unfulfilled. And there are those whose dreams seem simpler, more easily controlled by human efforts, but still aren't realized. Raising one's kids down the street from grandparents and aunts and uncles and cousins, for example, as they always hoped that they would.

I also found that sharing my story of loss served to encourage them. Not only did I feel a sense of "me too," they did also. The grief I internalized and was fearful to verbalize turned out to be something God used to build comradery.

AN ORIGINAL SISTER WIFE

If I had to compile a list of the "Top Five Most Heartbreaking Stories in the Bible," Leah's story in Genesis 29 and 30 would be among them. Her narrative is one heavy with grief over the loss of a dream.

There's no denying the personal dynamics in Leah's life are incredibly complex. Thanks to her father Laban's deceitful wedding night change of plans, she ends up the wife of a man who believed he was marrying her younger sister, Rachel. What further complicates the situation, though—as if it weren't already complicated enough—is that her new husband, Jacob, goes on to marry Rachel too. And, of his two wives, Rachel is the *only* one he loves. Scripture goes as far as to say that in her marriage, "Leah was hated" (Gen. 29:31).

I've often wondered why Laban was so eager to pawn Leah off on a man who hated her and yearned for her sister? Laban justifies his actions to Jacob with, "It is not so done in our country, to give the younger before the firstborn" (Gen. 29:26). But surely, in the seven years Jacob served Laban in order to marry Rachel, this father could have come up with another suitable husband for Leah. I'm left contemplating if in that culture, something as superficial as "weak eyes," which the writer of Genesis makes a point of saying Leah had, were indeed a deal breaker.

I don't know.

All I do know is that each time I read this story, I cringe. Jacob's reaction the morning after foretells what Leah's reality quickly becomes: a life of competition and jealousy fueled by rejection. One where she constantly vies for her husband's affection, only to find her efforts wasted.

There is the good news, though. In the midst of her disappointment, God doesn't forget Leah. While He never does turn her husband's heart toward her, He does open her womb. She goes on to mother six of the twelve tribes of Israel.

I find it fascinating to reflect, as Beth Moore writes, on how the names of each of Leah's sons reflect her emotional journey. She notes, "The statements Leah made are like mirrors reflecting her heart. They reveal a private process she experienced emotionally."[8]

At the birth of her first son, Reuben, whose name means "behold a son," Leah states, "Because the LORD has looked upon my affliction; for now my husband will love me" (Gen. 29:32). But sadly, Jacob still doesn't, and in response, Leah names her second son Simeon or "hearing," and states, "Because the LORD has heard that I am hated, He has given me this son also" (v. 33). By the time she births her fourth son, Judah, which means "praise," she's resolved that her baby-bearing isn't going to earn her Jacob's heart. At this boy's birth, she proclaims, "This time I will praise the LORD" (v. 35).

What Leah doesn't know at the time, is that the Master Storyteller has a special place in His narrative for her and the son who finally provokes her to stop looking to Jacob for affection and to Him instead. Robin Jones Gunn in her book *Victim of Grace* writes:

> Praise opens the door to a grateful spirit. Leah's situation didn't change. She changed. She chose to praise God and express that praise every time she said her baby boy's name— Judah. Praise.
>
> Did God delight in her change of heart? Did he bless her for turning her focus to him instead of continuing down her self-absorbed path of misery?
>
> Yes, he did. When God chose the family line through which his own Son would one day be born, he didn't choose Reuben, the firstborn, who traditionally received the blessing and birthright. . . . God chose Judah as the one from whose line the Messiah would come. Leah is one of the women in the line of Christ.[9]

I love that! While God could have established the lineage of Jesus through Rachel, the wife Jacob loved, He didn't. He chose Leah, the one who felt rejected and unwanted . . . the one who spent her entire life grieving a shattered dream.

I only wish that Leah had received some prophetic word, maybe even an angelic visitation, revealing this plan to her. But she didn't and her praise was short-lived. And it's this fleeting praise—not ultimately her father's deceitfulness or Jacob's refusal to love her—that makes Leah's story a tragedy. This true-life tale of hers epitomizes the very definition of the word "tragedy," a story "in which the main character is brought to ruin or suffers extreme sorrow, especially as a consequence of a tragic flow, moral weakness, or inability to cope with unfavorable circumstances."[10] Leah simply can't cope with her unfavorable circumstances.

In my own life, in those moments when that quiet sadness still comes, Leah's story doesn't simply remind me that I'm not the first to grieve the loss of a dream, but it also whispers to me, "Don't forget that it matters how you live out your story, unfulfilled aspirations and all." N. D. Wilson writes, "As it turns out, there is a difference between asserting that life is a story and actually living life like a story. And there is another difference between living life like a story and living life like a good story."[11] Leah didn't live her life like a good story—unless we're talking the melodramatic, soap opera variety— but I hope that I am and that I do.

LIVE A STORY OF LOSS WELL

How can you and I live out our lives like a good story, even as we grieve the loss of a dream? Here are some key attitudes I'm actively putting into practice.

An attitude of praise

At the birth of Judah, Leah chooses praise. She determines to focus her attention on God and His love for her. Leah makes an internal adjustment even though her external circumstances—namely, her marital relationship with Jacob—haven't improved. Unfortunately, as we saw, this attitude of praise doesn't last. It isn't long before she replaces those feelings of praise with the old status quo of misery.

And it's the practice of gratitude that can fuel our praise even when our story isn't what we anticipated.

While I've often done the same in the past, my future can be different. Yours can be too.

Look at Leah again. While I don't know for sure why praise doesn't stick for her, I do have a theory. It's this: Perhaps Leah didn't realize that praise isn't something we choose once and the attitude sticks forever. Rather, it's something we have to make a determined effort to adopt again and again *and* again. Day by day, hour by hour, and maybe even minute by minute.

And it's the practice of gratitude that can fuel praise even when my story isn't what I anticipated. I have to make a conscious effort to adjust my focus, to narrow in not on what God *hasn't* given me, but on what He *has* given me. Ann Voskamp captures this well when she writes, "To bring the sacrifice of thanksgiving means to sacrifice our understanding of what is beneficial and thank God for everything because He is benevolent."[12]

One practical way I try to fuel an attitude of praise is by often making a "What I'm thankful for today" list, and then praising God—out loud—for each item on the list. The more I exercise praise, the easier and more steadily it flows.

An attitude of remembrance

Leah's descendants also struggled with living out their lives as a good story. After their exodus from Egypt, the Israelites in the desert complained more than Dorothy when I serve summer squash for dinner. Like Leah, they lacked a continual attitude of praise. They were focused on all they'd lost in leaving Egypt, rather than all that God had done for them in the process. God's people failed to remember and express gratitude for His deliverance from Pharaoh and from slavery. They were only focused on the then and the now.

How did God seek to help them remain thankful? He encouraged them to have an attitude of remembrance.

In Joshua 4, we're given one illustration of this. We read that God instructs the Israelites to use twelve stones to construct a memorial in the middle of the Jordan River. Its purpose? To remind the twelve tribes—and their descendants—what God had done for them. Joshua says to them:

> In the future, your children will ask, "What do these stones mean?" Then you can tell them, "This is where the Israelites crossed the Jordan on dry ground." For the LORD your God dried up the river right before your eyes, and he kept it dry until you were all across, just as he did at the Red Sea when he dried it up until we had all crossed over. He did this so all the nations of the earth might know that the LORD's hand is powerful, and so you might fear the LORD your God forever. (Josh. 4:21–24 NLT)

God knew that His people were prone to forgetfulness, and that they needed visual reminders to keep praise in their hearts and on their lips.

I don't know about you, but I'm prone to forgetfulness too, especially when I'm feeling the deep sting of loss. And while I don't believe God wants me to ignore or bury my feelings of grief, but rather to process them in a healthy manner, I also believe He wants me to remember all that He's done for me in the past.

I do this by taking the time to ask myself some questions: In what ways has God been faithful to bring me through past losses? What beauty have I seen Him bring from the ashes in my own personal history?

Then, in those moments, I figure out a way to create my own visual reminders in the house, in the minivan, and any other space I spend a lot of time in. For me, this has included framing pictures of Ted and our daughters and hanging them in my walk-in-closet office space right next to my master's degree. These pictures serve as reminders that God's plan is often different than mine, but there is richness and beauty amid a dream unrealized.

An attitude of trust

When I purposely and regularly cultivate an attitude of praise and an attitude of remembrance, I find that an attitude of trust comes more easily. It's because the past faithfulness of God gives me hope for the future.

As I praise Him for all that He has done, and remind myself specifically of those things, the truth of Romans 8:28 (NLT) becomes more real to me. I see more clearly how God can and does cause "everything to work together for the good of those who love God and are called according to his purpose for them." Then, in those moments when things don't go as I plan, I'm more likely to trust that God has a plan I don't yet understand and, whatever that plan may be, it's good because He is good.

I DREAMED A DREAM

I'm currently teaching Dorothy to read a calendar. Each morning, we talk about what day of the week it is, which month, what the numeric date is, and the year. She still gets confused sometimes and tells me it's 2011. I jokingly tell her if that were the case, she'd still be a teeny, tiny baby. She can't help but giggle at the thought.

As I mentioned earlier, there are moments in my homeschool weekdays that are Instagram tidy and Facebook pretty. These are the instances when a new concept clicks for the first time or awe erupts at witnessing a successful science experiment. At the same time, we have math lessons that end in tears and English worksheets that mysteriously go missing. This reality of mine is beautiful, but also messy, not-at-all glamorous, and requires that I daily provide craft services.

Back when my fourteen-year-old self abandoned my early dreams of being a teacher and took up Hollywood aspirations, it's true that I never imagined myself teaching my kids full-time. I had no idea the journey of loss and grief God would take me on. What I also didn't imagine was how it would began to shape me for the better, providing me with the opportunity to connect with other women who, like me, also grieve the loss of a dream.

If you are one of those women, may you also find hope in believing that God knows every twist and turn of your story, from the first moment you dreamed a specific desire to the moments in which you've mourned it being left unfulfilled. While some of the bends in the road and the places He's taking you may not make sense or even be to your liking, I pray that like me, you too will discover some comfort in Him and in the "me too" of those around you.

CHAPTER 6

....

HEALTH

"Hope is necessary in every condition.
The miseries of poverty, sickness, and captivity would,
without this comfort, be insupportable."
—William Samuel Johnson[1]

The discomfort in my lower back woke me in the dark hours of predawn. I slowly and carefully shifted sleep positions, moving from my stomach to my side. No matter what nighttime posture I chose, though, the pain persisted.

Slowly, I crawled out of bed and shuffled to the couch, pausing only twice. First, to answer Ted's "Is everything okay?" inquiry, and second, to grab my laptop from the kitchen counter. Once seated, I did what I've heard one should never, ever, ever do.

I googled my health symptoms in an effort to self-diagnose.

If the Internet held answers on how to ease the relentless ache in my back, then it was well worth the risk of a dark collapse into what's called "cyberchondria," or the added anxiety that comes from attempting to identify physical woes using medical websites. The truth was, I was concerned it was appendicitis. But did appendicitis include back pain? I wasn't sure. I hoped the Internet could tell me.

Ten minutes later, I still didn't have any clarity. My online hunt revealed that a few of my symptoms—pain intense enough to wake me, nausea, and discomfort that had spread to include my abdomen—pointed to appendicitis, yet some of my other symptoms simply indicated it might be severe PMS.

I was at a loss.

I closed my laptop and stoically decided to wait it out. Perhaps given more time, the pain might decrease.

It didn't. Not even a little bit.

After an additional thirty minutes with no improvement, but only a worsening of the symptoms, my instincts instructed, "Go to the hospital."

I quietly, and painstakingly, got dressed and gently woke a sleeping Ted.

"What's going on?" he groggily asked. "Are you feeling any better?"

"Something's not right," I whispered. "This pain isn't normal. I'm going to drive myself to the hospital."

"Do you want me to drive you?" he asked, sitting up.

I silently weighed the options. One, we could wake up all four of our kids before dawn, dress them, pile them into the minivan, and drag them into the ER where they might potentially catch a communicable disease, or two, I could drive myself. The choice wasn't difficult.

"No," I responded. "I don't want to wake the kids and I really think I should go before the pain gets any worse."

Concern continued to etch its mark on Ted's face. "Are you sure? Do you think you *can* drive?"

"Yeah, I'm good. As long as I leave soon, I'll be okay."

A half hour later, I made it to the ER and within ten minutes they'd diagnosed me. I was the not-so-proud carrier of a kidney stone.

GOOD HEALTH INTERRUPTED

It's no secret that the condition of your and my personal health, whether good or bad, has the potential to affect all areas of our lives.

When we're able-bodied and strong, we feel more capable and better equipped to tackle our daily responsibilities. But if our physical, mental, or emotional wellness suffers, whether short-term or chronically, it's a struggle to fulfill our obligations and a chore to muster up the energy and strength to accomplish our normal to-do lists. At least, it is for me.

I've found that good health interrupted causes everyday life to suddenly become harder. Unmanageable at times, even. Some illnesses, such as my kidney stone or the intense 24/7 morning sickness I experienced during pregnancy, can transform even simple tasks such as brushing teeth or folding laundry into seemingly insurmountable mountains that feel impossible to scale. While my kidney stone only lasted a week, this tiny calcium buildup incapacitated me and forced me to neglect everything else.

I spent the week in bed, barely coherent. The medications prescribed to alleviate the intense pain muddied my thoughts and caused extreme drowsiness. I lacked the mental focus and physical ability to undertake my writing and editing projects, even the ones that cried "urgent" and demanded that I crawl out of bed and attend to them. I simply couldn't.

My title of homeschool mom was suspended. Our scheduled lessons were replaced with an impromptu fall break. Ted took vacation time to be both dad and mom to the kids and caretaker to me. He coordinated all the meals, drove me to the urologist, filled my prescriptions, and single-handedly managed bedtime duty for four girls each night. It was no small feat.

In those moments when I was lucid enough to fully grasp the havoc the kidney stone caused, a part of me mourned. I grieved the loss of the time, productivity, and accomplishment that a normal, sickness-free week provided. My Type A personality despised the mandatory rest and shuddered at the thought of falling behind in my work and in the girls' schooling.

With this sense of loss also came guilt. "You're not pulling your weight," Guilt whispered. "You're slacking and not contributing. You should be braver and stronger than this." Despite the indisputable fact that my physical condition was beyond my control, the shame of weakness and dependency plagued me.

Maybe you can relate to these sentiments all too well. Except for you, a kidney stone for a week or even morning sickness for a few months sounds easy compared to your health battle. It could be that you suffer from a chronic illness, perhaps diabetes or Lyme disease. Or maybe you've received a cancer diagnosis and your world feels like it's been turned upside down. If that's you, you aren't alone. My friend Rebecca understands.

BRAVING A HARD DIAGNOSIS

In early 2016, Rebecca was diagnosed with breast cancer. She shares what it was like to receive the hard news:

....

My heart knew immediately. I'd felt a lump, something foreign that would alter my course. After a mammogram, the radiologist counseled, "Brace yourself for hard news." Though her prediction stung, I'd already braced.

A flurry of biopsies and scans followed, leading us to an early morning meeting where my husband, Mark, and I found ourselves knee-to-knee with a specialist hovered around a pathology report and a breast diagram. Before the sun even got a chance to shine that day, the cancer diagnosis was official, the word "malignant" highlighted, and arrows drawn to the offending cells. The battle lines had been drawn, and it was time to pin on a pink ribbon and "fight like a girl."

I recognized immediately the first paradox of cancer. In an instant, I knew myself to be both a weakling and a warrior. I'd entered the breast cancer club, and there was to be a fight, one that would deconstruct the former me, physically, emotionally, and spiritually.

As Rebecca bravely entered the trenches of battle, she held firm to the belief that the Author of her story was good, even if her narrative now included the word "cancer." She notes:

The merciful news is that we do not fight alone, and all losses have their gains. We have a Great Healer, who pens redemption stories far more beautiful than any fleshly author ever could.

My first physical battle—and great loss—was a ten-hour surgery that involved a double mastectomy, reconstruction, and lymph-node removal. As Mark and I turned the corner into the hospital on surgery morning, we were bracing ourselves and being brave. But the Lord is ever and always in the details, always reminding us of His nearness, as there, at five a.m., stood three of my dearest friends. Their arms, their shared tears, and their prayers that day, offered me just enough strength to step into my hospital gown and walk into that operating room.

Surgery was just the beginning of the fight for Rebecca. Her battle with cancer continued to require courage as she mourned more loss.

After weeks of recovery, we found ourselves suspended before another pathology report, braced again for hard news, this time with an oncologist. More cells were offensive. More use of the word "malignant." There would be a year of chemotherapy, with four months involving some intense side effects.

I listened to the details, to words I'd always feared. I took notes on symptoms, never glancing at Mark for fear that any hint of tenderness would disrupt the flimsy hold I had on my raging emotions. But then she mentioned that my hair, my eyebrows, and my eyelashes would soon be counted as losses. I could do nothing but reach out for the hand of the man who would soon have a bald wife. As we made our way to the car, I let surrender be surrender, sobbed great heaving sobs, and allowed my husband to be the strong one.

I had a few weeks to wear ponytails or add curls. I had time to pretend that maybe it just might not happen. But then, one day, I realized my hairbrush was filled with hair; the prediction reality. By the next day, I was afraid to brush because large chunks were falling out in my hand. Strands covered my clothes, my sheets, my sink. Losing my hair shredded any final illusion of control I was gripping.

I had a choice to make. Watch it fall out in clumps or muster up some courage to take it all off at once with some intentional ceremony? I chose to shave it all off.

When the time came, I resisted the urge to chicken out. My courage was waning, so I invited friends for hand-holding purposes. Giggle therapy was also needed, so my kids grabbed hats from my new stash and made crazy faces. I was not to do this alone.

Mark plugged in his clippers and pumped worship music through headphones. When I nodded, the clippers buzzed on and I closed my eyes, anticipating the first cut. Then he clipped and shaved, and my hair simply fell to the ground around me, pieces of my former self falling away.

Our kids drew close, asking questions, praying over me, and offering tissues. It was my most vulnerable moment, and my daughter's hand held mine the whole time, giving me just enough courage for the moment.

We all cried, me sometimes with my head in my knees, for this new level of surrender, and for the whole journey from diagnosis, to surgery, to lost hair. The moment was sacred and sweet, tragic and powerful, and ceremonial because I needed for it to be.

When I finally looked into the eyes of my people, my head covered in short spiky hair that eventually fell out, I felt deep loss, but also unfathomable courage.

Then, we chose joy. My friends whisked me away from the hair covered floor, out for Pad Thai and giggles. This great loss was not without its gain.

The tears fell heavy that night, just as they have many times on this cancer road. But there was beauty, hope, deepened relationships, and weakness turned to strength by my Father's lavish love.

Malignant cells may have shaken me to my core, but there have been rays of bright light among the shards of glass. Vulnerability has stirred me to reach out beyond myself. I've desperately clasped my husband's hand in mine, felt my children's tender pats on my back when sick, and been carried on the shoulders of friends.

If God can help Rebecca bravely face cancer, in part through the love of family and friends, I believe He can do the same for us.

Most tenderly, I've cried out to the Lord, and He's been near again and again. I've freshly experienced the height and depth of His mysterious love. Though the cancer diagnosis caused me to brace, grasp for control, and begin calculating losses, the traversing of this road has taught me that sadness and sweetness, loss and gain, tend to walk in step.

Rebecca's story of pathology reports and difficult diagnosis wished untrue remind you and me that, as Joni Eareckson Tada writes, "Shared experiences ease the ache."[2] If God can help Rebecca bravely face cancer, in part through the love of family and friends, I believe He can do the same for us in whatever physical, mental, or emotional challenges interrupt our good health.

HOPE IS THICKER THAN BLOOD

The New Testament tells us the real-life tale of another woman who intimately understood what it was like to suffer a chronic illness, yet remain hopeful. Her account is recorded in three of the four Gospels,[3] and in all of them, she's unnamed. This anonymous woman is only identified by her sickness: an issue of blood.

We're told that she'd been hemorrhaging for twelve years. I can't imagine enduring a period that lasted for over a decade, yet *that* was this woman's daily reality.

What further complicated her situation is that in that culture and era, vaginal discharge translated to more than the need for a constant supply of feminine products. Not only was she physically ill, but according to Mosaic Law, she was also "ceremonially unclean."[4] Jewish law restricted her from public settings, and if she touched anyone, they became unclean too. As a result, the bleeding not only affected her physical body, it also impacted her relationships and impeded her mobility. She was most likely a shut-in because her chronic illness isolated her from society.

Understandably, this woman was determined to find a cure. In Mark 5:26, we learn that "she had suffered a great deal from many doctors, and over the years she had spent everything she had to pay them, but she had gotten no better. In fact, she had gotten worse" (NLT). Tragically, no one was able to help her.

No one, that is, until Jesus.

I can't help but think that for this woman, Jesus was her proverbial "Hail Mary." He was her last chance to be restored. Mark writes, "She heard about Jesus, so she came up behind him through the crowd and touched his robe. For she thought to herself, 'If I can just touch his robe, I will be healed'" (v. 27 NLT).

And just like that, she was.

Her hope—and her faith, Scripture notes—paid off. In that moment, her narrative changed; her suffering ended.

Let's not forget, though, that it took twelve years for her to reach that juncture, that turning point. There were twelve years of illness and suffering. Twelve years of isolation and social stigma. Twelve years of botched procedures and unending medical bills.

Perhaps your current situation is a twelve-year one too. Maybe not literally, but metaphorically. Like the woman with the issue of blood, prolonged illness plagues you. As a result, there've been weeks, months, even years of pain, isolation, and weariness. Or possibly your health struggle is a new one, and you're grasping to make sense of it. Whatever your present circumstances are, here are two encouragements we can all take away from this woman's story.

Put hope in God

On October 29, 1941, as war threatened to overwhelm Great Britain and fear grew palpable, Winston Churchill gave a speech to a group of boys at Harrow School in England. "Never, never, in nothing, great or small, large or petty, never give in,"[5] he admonished them. While the woman with the issue of blood lived centuries before Churchill uttered these words, she demonstrates for you and me what it means to never give in, even when it seems the odds are against us. Her story challenges us to place our hope—our full trust and reliance—in the eternal goodness of God, and not in the current discouraging condition of our physical bodies.

Think about her life up to this point. It would've been reasonable for this woman to have responded to Jesus with skepticism and cynicism. She'd already placed faith and confidence in multiple doctors and they'd all let her down. But she didn't. Instead, she approached Him with hopeful anticipation, and in doing so, she invited Him into her suffering. We can do the same.

Here's what I'm learning: when I muster the strength to rely on God during difficulty, I invite Him to share in my hardship, to fight alongside me as I battle fear and discouragement, pain and uncertainty. Joni Eareckson Tada, quoted earlier, became a quadriplegic as a result of a diving accident and knows well the pain of physical loss.

She explains:

> When you're in the trenches, handing bullets to your buddy and fighting a common enemy, hearts can't help but be pressed together. Your knowledge of each other is unique and intimate to you. . . .
>
> To know God in the trenches is to know why we trust him. Why shouldn't you trust the one covering your back in the crossfire? To know God is to be free of the incessant need to understand exactly what he is doing before you place confidence in him. Members with such *esprit de corps* are the happiest people in the world. . . .
>
> They know God will never run out of bullets—there will always be enough grace. They know God will never fail them. They know his mercy when they falter. His protection. His peace in the midst of the battle. His compassion for the hurting.
>
> They are convinced God is *with* them in the trenches.[6]

When we invest our hope in God regardless of whether our health improves or not, we can take some comfort in the truth that we don't brave our sorrow alone. Instead, I venture through suffering with a God who's described as "the Father of mercies and God of all comfort" and who is faithful to console "us in all our affliction" (2 Cor. 1:3, 4).

Reach out to others

A characteristic I love about the woman with the issue of blood is she wasn't passive. She didn't wait at home for Jesus to miraculously knock on her door. Instead, she left her comfort zone and reached out to Him.

Sure, her pursuit of Him was covert. She attempted to keep herself, her poor health, and the healing she anticipated a secret. At some level, though, I think she had to realize that her bold actions came with the risk of being caught and having her "unclean" condition revealed publicly. And, if she did understand that it *could* happen, this means her desire to put herself out there was ultimately stronger than her desire to remain hidden.

Her story reminds me, and hopefully you too, to be brave enough to reach out, not only to Jesus, but to others. I've already written a lot about why it's important for you and me not to isolate ourselves when we grieve. There was the "relational refugee" Rick from *Casablanca* who allowed the pain of past relationship loss to keep him from authentically engaging in community. I talked about Naomi who attempted to send her daughters-in-law back home, instead of grieving alongside them. There was Jesus' most infamous disciple Judas who, rather than return to his friends and repent of his betrayal, detached himself to the point of suicide. Lastly, there were my own stories. I shared my struggle to ask others for help when our air conditioner died, and how when it came to mourning the loss of my dream of being a television producer, I chose to do so alone out of fear.

But what does it mean to be brave enough to reach out like the woman with the issue of blood? It might be as simple as what I mentioned in chapter 4, and that's determining to have "twenty seconds of insane courage."[7] I'd say what this woman did certainly classifies as insane and courageous.

Courageously reaching out doesn't necessarily mean my life or yours becomes a tell-all book. We don't have to disclose our health losses on social media, to everyone we attend church with, or to all of our extended family, unless we want to. We can reach out and still exercise discretion, as well as maintain a level of privacy. What it does mean is that we don't conceal our suffering in a way that further isolates us from those closest to us. Rather, as Rebecca did, we invite them to pray for us, encourage us, and physically and emotionally be there for us.

To invite someone to share in our suffering requires sacrifice from us, though. It demands that we're open and honest with them about our condition and how it makes us feel, even if, like the woman with the issue of blood, we'd rather keep specifics hidden. It's practically impossible for a support system to support us if they don't have a clear view of what we're up against. When we choose to make our pain and suffering known and reach out to those we trust, we give them the opportunity to—as Jesus did for this woman—change our narrative. They may not be able to physically restore us, but they can walk with us and offer us strength to continue on. Don't forget: "Shared experiences ease the ache."[8]

THE HANDS THAT HOLD OUR LOVED ONES

With one hand, I steadied a ten-month-old Ava in my arms. With the other, I dialed 911.

Moments earlier, I'd been feeding her a bottle. For the last day or two, she'd battled a cold and a slight fever, but nothing too serious. That all changed suddenly, though, when she grew strangely still. Her eating paused and her eyes became fixed on the ceiling. I glanced up to see what had captured her attention, but nothing was obvious. It was then that her small body jerked.

Although I'd never witnessed a seizure firsthand, I was confident that she'd just had one. Urgently, I grabbed the phone. As I did, Ava's condition worsened. She stopped breathing, became unresponsive, and her color quickly faded to a troubling shade of blue.

I repeated her name over and over again as I waited for the emergency operator to pick up, hoping for some indication that my baby heard me. Nothing.

I'm not sure how long it took the operator to answer or how many times I uttered Ava's name. Thankfully, though, she finally started breathing again. Still dazed, she began to respond to my voice.

The doctor later concluded that she'd suffered a febrile seizure. These convulsions, which occur in only 4 percent of children under the age of five and don't continue throughout life, are caused by a fever that suddenly spikes. Fortunately, they're normally harmless, and in Ava's case this was true. She suffered only one additional febrile seizure about a month later and after careful examination was declared unaffected and perfectly healthy by both our pediatrician and a neurologist.

It's been over a decade since Ava's two seizures, yet I haven't forgotten how they made me feel: powerless. I understood at a new and profound level that whether my child lived or died wasn't ultimately up to me, and I hated feeling helpless.

Worry is often my way of exercising some form of control in an uncontrollable situation.

I'm confident that I'm not the only one who's felt this way. It's possible you have too. While you may not have a child who's specifically suffered a febrile seizure, you have experienced a sense of helplessness when it comes to the health of a loved one, whether it's a spouse, a child, a parent, or a close friend. It's painstaking and heartbreaking to watch someone we care deeply about suffer and not be able to ease their discomfort.

For a lot of us, the common response is to worry, to feel tormented or plagued with anxiety and concern. I have a tendency to not only obsess over the facts, but to also obsess over my assumptions about the facts and what they may mean for my loved one. As strange as it sounds, worry is often my way of exercising some form of control in an uncontrollable situation. It allows me to mentally and verbally dwell on what's happening, as I desperately grasp to find what the theater world terms a *deus ex machina,* or "a contrived solution to an apparently insoluble difficulty."[9]

Here's the thing, though, Scripture specifically instructs you and me *not* to worry. It's the exact opposite of what we're supposed to do. In Philippians 4:5–7, the apostle Paul writes:

> The Lord is at hand; do not be anxious about anything, but in everything by prayer and supplication with thanksgiving let your requests be made known to God. And the peace of God, which surpasses all understanding, will guard your hearts and your minds in Christ Jesus.

What I find interesting, not to mention convicting, about this passage is that before Paul tells us not to be anxious about anything, he very clearly reminds us: The Lord is at hand. God is here. He is with you and me. He's not absent from the situation and circumstances that tempt us to worry. Just like Jesus was with the disciples during the storm, He's with us in whatever "storm" we face.

Because the God of the universe is still in control, I don't need to find a *deus ex machina,* as much as I may long for one. Instead, I can and should let go of my anxiety and talk directly to Him about what concerns me. You can do the same. When we do, we're both promised a peace that we can't even fully understand.

LOVE LIKE A BRAVERMAN

We're not supposed to worry, but we are supposed to "encourage the fainthearted" and "help the weak" (1 Thess. 5:14). When those within our individual communities suffer health losses, it's our role as Jesus followers to be there for them.

One way I'm discovering I can do this is to love like a Braverman.

Two years ago, I Netflix-binged the NBC drama *Parenthood*. It chronicles the lives of three generations of the Braverman family. There's Zeek and Camille, their four grown kids, and, by the time the show ends, at least nine grandkids and a great-grandbaby too.

Over the course of six seasons, the Braverman clan celebrates engagements, weddings, pregnancy announcements, births, adoptions, and college acceptance letters. Simultaneously, though, they also brave the challenges of autism, teenage rebellion, unplanned pregnancy, abortion, marital separation, financial insecurity and, like my friend Rebecca, breast cancer. With each joy and each loss, the Bravermans are there for one another no matter what. They always show up. Plain and simple.

Parenthood brilliantly depicts what a supportive community can and should look like. Here are two specific lessons that the Bravermans demonstrate for me about being there for one another in health-related losses.

Family runs, not walks to help

When a member of the Braverman family ends up in the hospital, the other members flood the waiting room. They don't wait for an invitation to come. If an emergency happens that requires babysitting, there's no polite request needed for a sitter to volunteer, someone simply fills the need. Even the less reliable Bravermans are quick to help in some way, whether it's picking up a meal, assuming doggie daycare, or driving several hours to come to someone's rescue.

I can strive to do the same. It can be my goal to run—not walk—to help those in my community who face a health loss. Running requires that I sacrifice, though. The late author Kara Tippets, who died from cancer in 2015, explained:

> Nurturing friendships is hard enough when everyone is healthy. But when you show up and do the work of being a friend to someone who is suffering, it will cost you something. In other words, you're going to have to sacrifice your comfort, your schedule, and maybe even aspects of your faith.
>
> The last phrase may have caught you off guard. It is a little strange to think about sacrificing pieces of your faith. But consider it for a minute. If you've never really walked with someone through suffering, and if your view of God up to this point has resembled a math equation (prayer + God = healing), then I'm sorry to have to tell you, but you're going to have to sacrifice pieces of that way of believing.[10]

Through the Bravermans' onscreen example, I'm clearly reminded of the importance of being ready and willing to put the person I'm serving ahead of my own to-do lists, preferences, and even firmly held beliefs about how and when God chooses to relieve physical suffering. When it comes to healing, there isn't a simple equation.

As I help, though, I try to be mindful that if it's not an immediate family member or very close friend, to ask before I simply show up at the hospital or at their house. They may not have the energy for impromptu in-person visits. Instead, there are likely more practical ways they'd appreciate help, whether it's by providing a meal, financially contributing toward medical bills, or running errands.

Family doesn't let differences divide

In every season of *Parenthood,* there's at least one family member who commits a seemingly unforgiveable offense. It's an action, betrayal, or defiance that another Braverman swears they'll never get over. For several episodes, sometimes even an entire season, relational divide plays out. Yet, in the end, the Bravermans never allow anything to permanently divide them. On more than one occasion, reconciliation happens in the face of a health scare or other family crisis. In those moments of true emergency, the Bravermans once again run, not walk, to be there for each other. Loss always unites them.

I too can strive to ensure that differences don't divide me from those I love, especially when they need me the most. Proverbs 19:11 says, "A wise man restrains his anger and overlooks insults. This is to his credit" (TLB). The reality is all of us have differences with those closest to us at some point. It's tempting to hold on to disagreements when life gets hard, and use them as an excuse to not be there for each other. I'm trying not to let past or even present differences stand in the way of being there for a loved one facing a health crisis. Instead, as Romans 12:18 encourages me, "Do all that you can to live in peace with everyone" (NLT).

KIDNEY STONE REMINDERS

I wish I could confidently say my kidney stone days are behind me, but I can't. I've read that I'm now at a higher risk than people who've never before experienced one. There's the possibility I'll feel the excruciating pain and frustrating inconvenience of a second stone in the future. Honestly, I dread the possibility.

But if one day I *am* faced with another one, or a different health issue altogether, I pray that in the midst of the pain and the fear, I'll find strength and encouragement in what I've dubbed my "kidney stone reminders." Like the Israelites who constructed memorials to remind themselves of God's faithfulness to them when their lives where hard and discouraging, these reminders point me back to specific ways God faithfully and lovingly sustained me during this particular health struggle.

There was a husband who sacrificially stepped in to care for me.

There were friends who babysat for free.

There were small group members who dropped off comfort-food meals of honey-baked ham without anyone setting up a meal calendar.

Even though I alone bore the physical pain of the kidney stones, others carried me through it in every other way. For me, each individual was a much-needed evidence of a God who is attentively involved in even the hard aspects of my story.

As you bravely face your own difficult health struggles, I pray that you too will keep track of the ways both God and community are faithfully there for you, even in the hard times.

....

CHAPTER 7

LIFE

"Death doesn't discriminate
Between the sinners and the saints
It takes and it takes and it takes."
— Lin-Manuel Miranda[1]

The gel felt cold on my first trimester belly. I was too excited to care, though. We were about to eavesdrop on our fourth child and listen to his or her tiny heartbeat for the very first time.

As my nurse Kathy expertly moved the Doppler across my skin, my ears strained to catch that "galloping horse" sound among the static. It was the same sound we'd heard during my last three pregnancies, each of which had resulted in a full-term, healthy baby.

A minute passed, then two. There was nothing but empty noise.

"The heartbeat can be hard to find this early," Kathy assured us.

My concern grew as the minutes ticked on and she continued to seek the elusive gallop. Ted and I exchanged glances. When our obstetrician finally ushered us into the ultrasound room to "take a look," I knew something was wrong.

Through it all, a five-year-old Olivia was watching.

It was the first time we'd included one of our kids in the momentous "first heartbeat" appointment. It was also the first time there was no heartbeat to hear.

It was estimated that our baby, whom we later named Noah, had stopped growing at five weeks' gestation. That meant for thirty-five days, I was unaware that I was a walking tomb. I avoided caffeine, exercised with care, and jotted down lists of potential baby names, not knowing the youngest Slater's tiny body had ceased to grow within mine.

We went home that day numb. In the midst of our shock, we found ourselves assigned the difficult task of not only determining next steps as far as whether to miscarry at home or schedule a D&C, but of also walking our three young children through the death of a sibling they'd never met.

LIFE AS AN AMPUTEE

Noah's death isn't the only goodbye our family has said since Ted and I married in 2002. We've also mourned the passing of several grandparents, a few friends, and, most recently, Ted's dad.

If there's anything I've learned as I've grieved over the years, it's this: death permanently changes us. It never leaves us as it found us, nor does it politely refrain from affecting those things we hold as "normal" in our day-to-day life.

Death demands that we adapt and adjust to continue on without someone we love. How drastically our life changes, as well as the depth of our anguish, most often depends on the closeness of the relationship severed. It also depends on the physical pain we've witnessed our loved one endure, and how untimely and unexpectedly death's arrival has come.

In *A Grief Observed*, C. S. Lewis vulnerably writes about his life after the death of his wife. In it, he compares himself to an amputee:

> To say the patient is getting over it after an operation for appendicitis is one thing; after he's had his leg off it is quite another. After that operation either the wounded stump heals or the man dies. If it heals, the fierce, continuous pain will stop.

Presently, he'll get back his strength and be able to stump about on his wooden leg. He has "got over it." But he will probably have recurrent pains in the stump all his life, and perhaps pretty bad ones; and he will always be a one-legged man. There will be hardly any moment when he forgets it. Bathing, dressing, sitting down and getting back up again, even lying in bed, will all be different. His whole way of life will be changed. . . . At present I am learning to get about on crutches. Perhaps I shall presently be given a wooden leg. But I shall never be a biped again.[2]

Lewis captures well the fact that death isn't something we'll simply "get over" with time. Rather, we're required to painfully endure the changes it brings as we slowly learn to live with our loss.

My friend Keri, whose husband Scott tragically died in a car accident in 2015, has also found this to be true. She says, "There is nothing anyone can do to prepare you for the shock when you get that fateful knock at the door. I woke up that Monday morning a married woman and went to bed that night a widow with a five-year-old and a two-month-old to raise." She notes, "When my husband died, part of me changed. I found that people expected me to be the same, especially after months and then a year passed. Grief has no timetable or prescription. Grief doesn't magically end one day."

Because grief *is* something you and I have to learn to live with, how can we come to navigate life after the death of a loved one? While not all approaches may work for everyone, here are three things that I've found beneficial in my own grief. Perhaps you'll find them helpful too as you mourn.

Determine to trust the Author

Deciding to put my trust in the Author of my story is something about which I've shared a lot. To rely on God requires that I *actively* choose to do so. The death of someone I love makes this more painful because it's natural amid loss to question whether God sees me and cares about me. After all, if He does, why would He have permitted my loved one to die and why is He allowing me to experience such despair? Is He *really* writing a good narrative for me?

Trusting God doesn't mean I don't have questions, and it certainly doesn't mean I can't voice them. God can handle my "whys." Following the miscarriage, I had doubts about the purpose and effectiveness of prayer.

Before Noah was conceived, I had prayed for another baby. After the pregnancy test revealed a positive result, I asked regularly for a healthy, full-term infant. Objectively, my prayers didn't work. They were ineffective. So why should I bother to pray? Did it really matter in my life?

I shared this with Ted and he responded with something I'll never forget. "Prayer is about relationship," he reminded me. As hard as it was to accept this, I knew he was right.

I shouldn't pray because I want God to give me everything I want, although prayer does include petition. When Jesus taught His followers to pray in Matthew 6, He instructed them to ask that their daily needs be met. Paul, in his letter to the Philippians, also points to prayer as a way to "present your requests to God" (Phil. 4:6 NIV). In the end, though, when God doesn't respond to one of my appeals in the way I hope, it shouldn't devastate my prayer life. It needs to be based on connection with God, not on what He may or may not give me.

Being unafraid to wrestle with these questions served to deepen my relationship with God. I was reminded that trust isn't about my character or who I am. It's about God's character and who He is, and as we've already discussed in chapter 5, Scripture tells us that He is "the Father of mercies and God of all comfort, who comforts us in all our affliction" (2 Cor. 1:3–4).

I can decide to base my trust not on the pain I experience, but on the fact that God loves me and promises to be "near to the brokenhearted" and those "crushed in spirit" (Ps. 34:18). For me, determining to trust the Author of my story, even when it's devastatingly hard, has been an important step in learning how to live with loss.

Allow others to see the real you

"Never let them see the real Elizabeth Windsor," Winston Churchill instructs a young Queen Elizabeth II in Netflix's Golden Globe Award–winning series *The Crown*. "The cameras . . . the television . . . never let them see that carrying the crown is often a burden. Let them look at you, but let them only see the eternal."[3]

There have been times I've been tempted to give myself a similar speech. Except the burden I've borne wasn't leadership, but grief. In these moments, there's been self-inflicted and sometimes even outside pressure for me to bravely focus on the eternal and spiritual aspects of death and not allow others to see human weakness, brokenness, and questioning.

The good news is, I'm not Elizabeth Windsor, and I don't have to courageously present myself as strong or hide the real me as I mourn. Jesus Himself grieved the pain of death openly, and His example frees me to do the same.

In John 11, Jesus receives word that His friend Lazarus is ill. Lazarus's sisters, Mary and Martha, beg Jesus to come quickly and heal their brother. Yet Jesus delays, and by the time He finally does arrive, He's informed that Lazarus has been buried for four days. His beloved friend is dead.

His other friends Mary and Martha are beside themselves with grief and asking why He didn't come sooner. What is Jesus' response? Scripture tells us, "Jesus wept" (John 11:35).

Here's the interesting thing, though, Jesus had the power to quickly turn His friends' sorrow into joy. He could have skipped the tears, told His friends to "get over their grief," and moved directly to the raising of the dead. But He didn't.

Instead, Jesus takes a moment to publicly reveal an important part of who He is: His empathetic nature. I love how Brené Brown explains empathy. She says, "Empathy is not feeling for somebody. It's feeling with them. It's touching a place in me that knows where you've been so I can look at you and say, 'Me too, Brother. You're not alone in this.'"[4] This is what we see Jesus express as He weeps in this moment.

In doing so, Jesus not only demonstrates His empathetic nature, but He also models for me that allowing myself to feel the sting of death and to disclose it without inhibition is not a shortcoming. It is not a weakness. He gives me permission to show the real me as I mourn.

Freely expressing the weakness and brokenness I feel may not free me from sorrow, but it does help lighten my burden as I navigate a "new normal."

Seek outside counsel and help

For over twenty years, my dad has worked as a hospice chaplain. He's helped individuals and families walk through the painful process of death and dying. Through his work with those left behind, he's demonstrated for me that I don't have to learn to live with loss on my own. It's okay to seek out others to help me navigate life as I now know it.

What can this outside counsel and help look like for me and for you too?

One, it could be a close friend. Throughout this book, I've talked about surrounding ourselves with at least one or two individuals whom we trust. I mentioned in the prologue that Shauna Niequist calls these people our "home team."[5] These are family members or friends who allow us to speak without censorship and cry without rebuke.

Two, many churches have ministries aimed at helping people process grief. For example, our church has what's called "Stephen Ministry." It's made up of highly trained individuals who walk through loss one-on-one with those who are grieving. You can call your church office or talk to someone on staff to see what your church offers.

Three, there are professional counselors who specialize in grief. They can offer you and me a safe place to vulnerably share, as well as help to expertly guide you through the loss. If you're not sure where to find one, websites like FocusontheFamily.com and the American Association of Christian Counselors (AACC.net) offer counseling referrals.

Determining to trust the Author, allowing others to see the real me, and seeking outside help are three ways I've slowly made sense of life after the death of a loved one. They may be helpful to you too as you mourn.

But what if you and I aren't the one who is deeply grieving right now? How can we be there for someone we know or love who is? One way is to practice remembrance.

THE IMPORTANCE OF REMEMBRANCE

I'll never forget answering the phone one March morning in 2004 when I was seven months pregnant with Olivia. It was our small group leader from church.

"Ashleigh," he said. "There's been an accident."

He informed me that a friend of ours and her preborn son had tragically died in a car accident the night before.

I hung up the phone in shock, and slowly walked upstairs to wake Ted. He'd been friends with her, her husband, and her family for years.

While I hadn't known them as long as Ted had, I did identify closely with her. She and I had been married almost the same amount of time. We were both expecting our first child within weeks of each other. Just a few days earlier, we'd even discussed baby shower dates. Much like Leslie's death in *The Bridge to Terabithia* had given Olivia a heightened awareness that the world wasn't as safe or as fair as she'd once believed, our friend's death reminded me that we aren't promised tomorrow.

Ted and I desperately struggled to process their deaths. But, we weren't sure where to start. I turned to my dad, the hospice chaplain, for guidance. He talked me through my sorrow, comforting and encouraging me.

I confided in him that I felt at a loss on how to best convey empathy to our friend's husband and family. What should I say or not say? How could I help? Would the presence of my large-with-child belly add further pain?

He offered me a nugget of wisdom that I carry with me to this day. It was this: grief is a long-term process, but we often forget that's the case when we're not the ones most directly affected by the loss. Simply put, long-term remembrance is important.

From our discussion, I learned that in the initial stages of sorrow, there's typically a large outpouring of love, support, and sympathy from one's community. There are services devoted to honoring and remembering the life of the one who died. Cards are written, financial donations offered, and casseroles baked. We all earnestly rally around the grieving spouse, children, parents, or siblings. With time, though, it's likely that those of us outside the family and close circle of friends begin to move on. The delivery of meals stops, the phone calls and emails become less frequent. Everyone else returns to their normal, day-to-day lives. As this happens, we may stop acknowledging someone else's amputee status, forgetting that there is no returning to "normal" for them.

This conversation with my dad taught me that one of the best ways to offer ongoing love and support is to reject forgetfulness and choose remembrance instead.

Practice long-term honor of an individual's life

You and I can actively honor someone's memory long-term. While we may believe that with time it's better to reminisce less often in an effort to spare those who are grieving prolonged pain, silence can be hurtful unless its specifically requested. Our self-censorship may be fueled by good intentions, but the problem is that when we don't practice remembrance it has the potential to communicate, "You should be over your loved one by now." On the other hand, when we choose to recall our fond memories of the person who's died, we validate that an individual and the impact they made still matter.

There's a song titled "For Good" in *Wicked*, the Broadway musical that tells the story of *The Wizard of Oz* from the Wicked Witch's perspective. In it, two of the characters sing about how each has affected the other's life for good. On more than one occasion, Ted has told me it's a song he wants sung at his funeral one day. He hopes that others will say, "My life is changed because I knew Ted Slater." Just like Ted wants others to reflect positively on his life, those left behind need to know that they aren't the only ones who've been changed for good by the person they've lost.

My friend Julie beautifully shares the importance remembrance plays for her and her family as they honor the life of her son, Leyton.

....

The boyish face of a young man with solemn, gentle eyes flashed across my news feed. His name was Shai Kushner—a twenty-year old soldier in the Israeli Defense Force who was killed fighting near the Gaza border.

Under his picture were the words "Zichro l'brakhah." In Hebrew, it means, "May remembering him be a blessing."

I love that.

It made me think of our firstborn son. He, too, died. I was pregnant with him and his twin sister and at twenty-eight weeks in the womb, he unexpectedly twisted on his umbilical cord. Doctors couldn't find his heartbeat, though his sister's remained steady. I cried all the way up to the larger hospital I was being sent to, to await their birth. Four weeks later, my little girl and boy were delivered together—one alive and the other dead.

We named him Leyton, our precious boy whose first embrace was in the arms of Jesus. We named her Lauren, our sweet girl who struggled for several months in the hospital and is now, by God's grace, a healthy eleven-year-old. We love them both. We miss him, still.

Every year on the anniversary of Leyton's death, "Heaven Day," as we call it, we head to the same solitary, dirt road in the mountains. We cry, release baby blue-colored balloons and eat birthday cupcakes. It is a sacred place off the beaten path where we talk about Leyton and the reality of heaven. On that day, we do something we think he would love if he were here. One year, we went to a dinosaur museum—a perfect outing for a little boy. Another time, we went to a train exhibit and still another year, we went mini-golfing, and on another, we hiked a mountain trail.

Remembering is an important part of our grieving process, but it is also a declaration of the truth about who we are and Whom we belong to.

To remember is to lay hold of our true worth. Leyton is not a faded memory or an unpleasant incident in our history. The purity of his value is not reduced by tragedy or sorrow. Created in the likeness of God Almighty. Beloved before time. Unforgettable and treasured long after this world has passed. He is a living member of our family—more alive than we are now and safely in the arms of Jesus just as we will be some day.

Isaiah 43:4 captures the heart of God toward each one of us, "You are precious in my eyes, and honored, and I love you."

This truth cannot change though the location of our physical bodies eventually will and it is one that bears remembering each and every day.

To remember is to press in to the father heart of God. Those who grieve are painfully familiar with the "Aren't you over that?" question. Most have never thought of applying the same sentiment to God though.

Take, for example, the parable of the Prodigal Son found in Luke 15. What if, instead of a loving father longing for the return of his wayward son, Jesus depicted a dismissive, detached dad? When a friend asks the prodigal son's father how he's doing, he'd speak awkwardly and only about his remaining son. No tears for the missing one. No aching heart and no longing gaze toward the dusty road—only suppression of memory and heart.

But this is not the father Jesus spoke of.

The clear picture is of a father who cannot forget. His mind is never far from his child. Even his body longs for him. He aches for reconciliation and his spirit overflows with joy when he sees the far away speck that is his son down the long, dusty road.

The parable is a true depiction of God's heart and He is never "over" us. There is a place for each one of us that no one else can take.

I love Isaiah 49:15–16, "Can a woman forget her nursing child, that she should have no compassion on the son of her womb? Even these may forget, yet I will not forget you. Behold, I have engraved you on the palms of my hands."

He never forgets, for He cannot.

So when my heart turns toward my beautiful boy with chestnut hair like mine and a turned out nose like his daddy's, I remember. I remember the wonder of Leyton, the priceless, unfading value of his life. I remember the God who cannot and will not forget him or me. Our very names are engraved upon His own hands. And that is good. It is a blessing. For that is what Leyton is.

....

Julie's not the only one to testify to the importance of remembrance. Jenny Schroedel, Bereavement Services Coordinator at Hospice of Kona on the Big Island of Hawaii, shared with me, "In grief counseling, we almost never use the word 'closure.' That word suggests some kind of tidy, perfect end. Instead, we say that the conversation never ends. We say that it is okay, great even, to write letters to your loved one, to remember who they were to you, to gaze at their photo. It is from these places of connection that we draw strength and find courage to move forward, not away from the loss, but into the future with the loss, bearing it as we can and learning from it as we go."

When we choose to remember alongside the person who is grieving most deeply, we can play a part in helping them find, as Jenny says, the strength and courage to move forward.

Practice long-term acknowledgment of grief

Choosing remembrance requires a long-term commitment to acknowledge and be sensitive to someone's grief. Jenny explains:

....

The poet David Whyte compares the experience of grieving to falling in love, except that when you are falling in love you are falling toward a person, but when you are grieving you just fall and fall and fall. And you often don't know what you are falling toward. But what you are falling toward is the ground that other person held for you. When you can fully see who they were to you and what they meant to you, it is from this ground that you can rebuild.

All this takes time. And this is extremely frustrating to many of my clients, who often ask (with some amount of desperation) how long they will feel like this. I can only tell them that it will usually take longer than they think it might, but that the grief changes as they move through time. They may never fully let it go, and that is okay, but in time, they learn to carry it more lightly.

....

Even as time helps grief become lighter, sorrow can still resurface abruptly and unexpectedly. Today, the "On This Day" memory that Facebook chose to show me was a picture of Savannah wearing an "I'm a Big Sister" T-shirt. It was the public announcement we'd made for my pregnancy with Noah back in 2010. Despite the years that have passed, the sight of it still hurt. But it's not just social media that can cause grief to resurface. It can also occur at the sound of a favorite song on the radio, when driving past an old haunt, or on calendar dates that hold great importance such as wedding anniversaries, birthdays, and holidays.

When it comes to significant dates, we can actively take the time to recognize them. This may include sending a card, making a phone call, or even treating someone to lunch. On holidays, we can check in to make sure they aren't spent alone.

For a single mom like Keri, remembrance also includes offers to meet day-to-day needs. "The pain and stress of grief, and the challenge of finding myself a single mother, left me with practical needs that I had neither the time nor the energy to take care of," she explains. "If you can help clean house, prepare food, provide childcare, do so. And not just for the first few weeks. Grief doesn't stop after a few weeks."

Practicing long-term acknowledgment is a way we can help someone who's grieving feel less alone in their sorrow. It's a concentrated effort on our part to continually communicate, both in word and action, that we see them, we remember them, and we love them.

TWO WAYS TO INDIVIDUALIZE REMEMBRANCE

Are there also specific things you and I can do to help us practice remembrance in a way that better caters to what a particular individual may need? Absolutely. We can strive to understand, respect, and support the unique way he or she mourns, which includes honoring the "how" and the "when" of their grief.

Understand "how" someone grieves

While it's true that the death of a loved one permanently changes each of us in some manner, it's also true that we don't all respond to grief in exactly the same way. As I touched on briefly when I discussed job loss, our individual personalities affect how we react to loss and express sorrow.

For example, I'm what you might call a "full immersion" griever. I don't shy away from the deep emotional ache of loss and how it impacts me. I allow myself to intensely feel the onslaught of assaulting emotions, from denial and anger to bargaining and depression. I cry regularly and easily, and I freely express to others exactly what I'm feeling.

Ted, on the other hand, engages loss less emotionally. His tendency is to "do" in response to grief rather than "feel." For him, there's less questioning and less emotional turmoil. Sorrow fuels action and acceptance comes more quickly. I witnessed this in his reaction to his dad's death. His first instinct wasn't to gauge his own emotional state; instead it was to actively find ways to comfort and assist his stepmom.

While Ted's and my differing ways of expressing sorrow certainty aren't the only ways that people grieve, they offer two distinct examples of how someone may respond to the loss of a loved one, both immediately and even long-term.

In what way does understanding how someone grieves help with remembrance?

It better equips you and me to be there for them in a helpful and encouraging manner. We realize that if they are a "full immersion" griever, they may need us to simply let them emote without judgment or question. Most likely, they'll want to reminisce about their loved one often. While others grow weary of entering their grief by engaging in conversations about the person who's died, we can continue to "talk story," as they call it in Hawaii. Or, if we understand that they channel their grief into action, we'll be the first to join them in a cancer charity walk every year or encourage the new hobby they take up that reminds them of their loved one.

For me, in order to better support my friends who've also experienced miscarriage, I've had to learn to understand that not all moms mourn it in the same way I did, specifically when it comes to including their other children in the grief process. As I mentioned, Ted and I actively involved our kids, but not all families do. Many parents decide not to.

Honestly, I don't blame them. After all, miscarriage is a complex loss to mourn. It involves the death of an unseen, never-before-met member of the family whose existence often hasn't even been shared with small children if it's not yet the second trimester. There are no memories with this tiny person, no concrete reminders that he or she even existed, such as clothes or toys or pictures. Trying to explain to a young child what it means for a preborn sibling to die results in tough questions. The morning of my D&C, I remember a four-year-old Ava asking, "Mama, how can Noah be in two places at once?" She didn't understand how Noah's body could still be "in my tummy," while his or her spirit was with God.

Even so, for Ted and me, grieving with our kids felt natural and necessary. Yet, I've realized and accepted that it doesn't feel this way for all parents. As a result, I don't expect or put pressure on others to do exactly as we did. Instead, I respect and support their desire and need to mourn the loss of their preborn baby in their own way.

Respect "when" someone grieves

Just as we don't all respond to grief in the same manner, we don't all process it at the same speed either. When it comes to the five stages of grief—denial, anger, bargaining, depression, and acceptance—some of us may linger in one stage longer than others. Part of choosing to respect "when" someone grieves means allowing them to mourn at their own individual pace. We briefly touched on this when we talked about job loss.

But why is it vitally important not to rush the grieving process for others? Jenny notes, "Almost daily my clients tell me that others are pushing them to 'get over it' or 'move on.' I always tell them that there is a time to simply be present to the reality of a death. It takes time to feel it, to grieve it, to fully see how this loss has changed you. Paradoxically, studies show that those who are pushed to move on grieve longer than those who are encouraged to take the time they need."

An important part of respecting "when" someone grieves is being careful with our words. Keri notes, "Don't tell your loved one that he or she will find someone else, or if they had a child pass away that they can have another one. I was told twice that I was young and could remarry before we even had the funeral, and several times more in the last year and a half. There are no words, no logic, that can soothe the grieving heart," she explains. "Don't try to find the words to say that right thing because most likely you will end up saying the wrong thing. If you have to say something, don't underestimate the power of a simple, 'I love you.'"

To clarify, not rushing someone doesn't mean we shouldn't be acutely aware of another's emotional state as they mourn. Some personalities are more prone to contemplate suicide in their sorrow.

What are some suicide warning signs of which to be aware? The American Foundation of Suicide Prevention notes they can be present in an individual's mood, talk, and behavior. Someone who's considering suicide may exhibit severe depression, anxiety, irritation, or even rage. Talk may include statements about "being a burden to others, feeling trapped, experiencing unbearable pain, having no reason to live, [and] killing themselves," while behavior may feature substance abuse, reckless actions, withdrawal and isolation, sleep issues, saying goodbye to loved ones, and aggression.[6]

If you and I notice that a grieving friend or family member seems to have hit a concerning and dangerous low, we should be ready and willing to intervene and make sure they get professional help.

It's true that you and I can't remove someone else's grief. We can't magically make everything better for them. What we can do is to purposefully and lovingly help them feel less alone in their sorrow as we actively remember them and the loved one they've lost.

OPEN CASKET CAMARADERIE

When Ted's dad died, we rented a minivan and drove from Atlanta to Wisconsin for his funeral.

His viewing marked the first time our four girls stood at an open casket. Each of them responded differently. Their unique personalities and even ages impacted how they reacted to seeing the earthly body of their once full-of-life grandpa now asleep.

I'll never forget watching Dorothy, who was five at the time. Of all the girls, she was the most curious, and had the least experience with death. I remember her standing next to Grandma, who encouraged her to gently touch Grandpa's hand. In that moment, Dorothy shied away. She wasn't yet ready.

Later, though, I caught a glimpse of her standing alone at his coffin. I watched as she glanced to the left, to the right, and behind her. When she was confident no one was looking, she reached her small hand out and quickly touched her grandpa's fingers. Curiosity had driven her to see what death felt like. Yet, she wanted to do it privately and on her own, without notice. She didn't realize that both Grandma and I saw her.

The next day at the funeral, Ted and I invited Dorothy to join us at the coffin again. Ted had heard of her curiosity the day before, so he reached out and touched his dad's hand too. He wanted to let her know that her actions were okay. With this, he offered her a "me too." He communicated to our girl, "I'm struggling to process this too. Let's brave it together."

Whether we're the one personally and devastatingly grieving the death of a loved one or the one supporting someone who is, there's power in "me too." I love what Helen Keller, who knew loss well, once wrote. She said, "We bereaved are not alone. We belong to the largest company in all the world—the company of those who have known suffering. When it seems that our sorrow is too great to be borne, let us think of the great family of the heavy-hearted into which our grief has given us entrance, and, inevitably, we will feel about us their arms, their sympathy, their understanding."[7]

EPILOGUE

*"Heaven will solve our problems, but not, I think,
by showing us subtle reconciliations between all our
apparently contradictory notions. The notions will
all be knocked from under our feet. We shall
see that there never was any problem."*
— C. S. Lewis[1]

Gray shrouded the Colorado sky that particular Saturday morning in May 2010. Rain had fallen sporadically throughout the week and, as the color of the heavens hinted, threatened to continue into the weekend.

"How soggy do you think the grass is this morning?" I asked Ted, as he grabbed a bag of coffee beans from the pantry.

"Probably not too bad," he replied. "Why?"

"Maybe we could take the girls to visit Noah's grave today," I said.

Ted paused. "I woke up with the same thought. Really. I did."

In stories of first-trimester miscarriages, a gravesite isn't a topic often discussed. Many preborn babies, whose young lives end early in the first month or two of pregnancy, aren't given a formal, physical resting place here on earth. Our story was different, though. It did include a cemetery, a headstone, and a grave.

Two days after the ultrasound revealed Noah had died, my body began to miscarry on its own. I lacked the emotional and physical fortitude necessary to say goodbye to my baby at home, as many of my friends have courageously done. So instead, my personal rendition of *brave* involved an emergency D&C. It was a different kind of hard, but hard all the same. Rather than being aware of my child's physical separation from me, I fell asleep pregnant and woke up postpartum.

There was a moment prior to the procedure that holds permanent residence in my memory. It was the moment when our nurse handed Ted and me a form that explained our options regarding Noah's body. Regardless of how sensitively something like this is handled, there's no erasing when someone asks you what you'd like done with your dead child's remains, no matter how small or still forming those remains are. A moment like this changes you in ways you can't possibly imagine beforehand.

Of the options, we chose to have Noah buried in a community memorial alongside other preborn babies who had died. This service was offered to us at no charge, as a gift from a local Catholic diocese. It provided us the opportunity to have something tangible that testified of Noah's existence and impact on our lives.

As Ted and I chatted that Saturday morning in May, it had been weeks since we'd made the first visit to the cemetery, just the two of us. It was a trip marked by deep sorrow and the longing to lay my body prostrate on the fresh dirt and weep. I mourned the physical body I'd never nurture.

When it came time to leave, all my mother bear instincts made me reluctant to go. For me, to walk away felt like abandonment. It meant to turn my back on what had once been my child's fearfully and wonderfully made frame; one I'd only seen the small shadow of on an ultrasound. Only a month earlier, my body had protected it; now it was sheltered merely by a small coffin and layers of dirt.

Ted sensed my struggle. "Noah's not really there," he told me. "It's okay to leave."

He was right. As we'd explained to Ava the morning of the D&C when she'd questioned, "Mama, how can Noah be in two places at once?" Noah's spirit lived on. The eternal part of our child was alive, whole, and happy in the presence of a strong, tender, and compassionate God. Noah may have never run or jumped or giggled with us, but I had no doubt that's exactly what our child was doing in the eternal presence of our loving Father.

I don't know about you, but for me, loss, more than anything else, causes me to reflect on heaven. It serves to remind me that the hardship and difficulty I experience here is temporal, but the stories God is writing for me, you, and even Noah are everlasting. Even when our bodies fail us, as Noah's did, our spirits live on.

This truth doesn't diminish or lessen the pain I feel, or wrongly provoke me not to grieve. As I've talked about throughout this book, it is healthy and right to mourn. I don't ever let anyone convince me otherwise. Every loss you and I experience, and the pain we suffer as a result, is worthy of mourning.

Heaven, though, gives us hope. It gently whispers: loss is not a forever part of your story. We're promised that one day we'll be reunited with those we love in a place where the Author of all of our narratives wipes away every tear from our eyes. A place where "death shall be no more, neither shall there be mourning, nor crying, nor pain anymore" (Rev. 21:4). It's here that all of us who mourn the loss of home will fully feel the belonging, the inclusion, and the safeness we so deeply desire.

A few months ago we celebrated Ted's dad's birthday. It was the first birthday since he bid us farewell for the other side. Ted, who was traveling with Ava at the time, texted me, "I heard a song this morning that made me think about Noah . . . and then I thought that my dad may have met him or her." His words testified to an important truth.

Not only is my story and yours never ending, but community is too. Relational unity with other Jesus followers is eternal. Heaven is a place where we will finally fully experience relationship with God and others as it was originally intended. It's like Allison mentioned in chapter 2 as she reflected on her relationship with her mom. "At the end of our lives here on earth," she noted, "my mom and I are both daughters of God and we will spend our lives together eternally—free of conflict, full of acceptance."

On that Saturday morning in May, Ted and I drank coffee and decided to make our second visit to Noah's grave. This time we brought our baby's three big sisters with us. As the sun emerged and the grayness lifted, we led them to the spot. With curiosity they studied it, asked more questions, and carefully laid pictures and letters they'd written for their lost sibling next to the headstone.

They soon took to running in the grass, chasing butterflies, and admiring flowers lovingly left by others. While they did, I sat down next to the community memorial and felt a sense of camaraderie like never before. The gravestone was surrounded by baby toys, flowers, and notes left by other bereaved parents and their families. I found myself praying for these other moms and dads who walked a similar road of grief. I asked that God would comfort them, and that when they visited this spot, they too would experience His comforting presence.

"God's in His heaven, all's right with world," Anne Shirley says in *Anne of Green Gables*.[2] When you and I experience loss, it often feels like this couldn't be further from the truth. Yet when we choose to brave sorrow, together, allowing faith to transform us and our community to uphold us, we can courageously echo these words, believing that the Author of my story, and your story, is with us even when life is hard and the world feels anything but right.

THE WHY AND HOW OF COMMUNITY

For some of you, diving into community comes easily. You're like my outgoing and fearless daughter who makes a new friend no matter where she goes. For others of you, though, building relationships is a slower process. You're more like my girl who's quiet and reserved. It takes her longer to establish strong connections.

Regardless which of my daughters you more closely identify with, there's one thing we all have in common when it comes to community. We all crave it at some level. There's something in each of us that desires to have, as Shauna Niequist writes, "middle-of-the-night, no matter what people."[1] These are the people who celebrate our victories with us and deeply mourn our losses.

Why is it that we long for relational connection? Scripture provides us with answers.

GOD HIMSELF IS IN COMMUNITY

In Genesis 1:26, God says, "Let us make man in *our* image, after *our* likeness" (emphasis mine). This is our first indication in Scripture that God isn't a solitary being. It's our introduction to the Trinity, the concept that we serve a multifaceted Creator who makes Himself known in three persons: the Father, the Son, and the Holy Spirit.

Throughout the Bible, we find more references to the triune nature of God. Take 2 Corinthians 13:14 (NLT), for example, where Paul writes, "May the grace of the Lord Jesus Christ, the love of God, and the fellowship of the Holy Spirit be with you all."

God Himself lives in constant community, in continual fellowship with Himself. He knows intimately the value and importance of community and, as we see next in Genesis, He wants us to experience it too.

GOD DECLARED OUR NEED FOR COMMUNITY

"It is not good that man should be alone," God proclaims six days into creation.[2]

He's just finished His *magnum opus artificis*, or greatest work as an artist. This is where, as you'll remember from our discussion of relationships, God literally got His hands dirty and formed Adam from dirt.

Even though Adam lives in perfect friendship with his Maker, God determines that this first man needs human community too. In this, God—not us—declares our need for close, authentic relationships with others.

Several thousands of years later, during His earthly life and ministry, Jesus reinforces this idea that "it's not good for man to be alone." Even though He's God made man, Jesus doesn't choose a solitary life. He's purposeful to live in community with other people. He intentionally chooses a group of twelve close friends, or disciples, and "does life" with them. They travel together, pray together, minister together, and literally face stormy seas together. Scripture also notes He has dear friends outside His circle of the Twelve, which include Mary, Martha, and Lazarus.

Simply put, we need community because God tells us that we do. He not only verbally proclaimed it following His creation of Adam, but He modeled it for us in Jesus.

JESUS MODELED HOW TO "DO" COMMUNITY

What does Jesus' example teach us about the "how" of community? Here are a couple of important truths we can glean from His life.

Community isn't a grand-scale event

"You only need to have one or two close friends," I tell my quiet and reserved daughter. She's not a person who feels comfortable and at ease in large groups; she prefers more intimate settings, which allow for talk that goes beyond that of small.

The good news for her and for many of you is that Jesus demonstrates that living in community doesn't have to be a grand-scale event. He had masses who followed Him, yet He chose to only have close friendships with a few. Even within His twelve disciples, He had three buddies—Peter, James, and John—He was closest to. These are the friends He took with Him during His transfiguration[3] and the ones He asked to watch with Him in the garden of Gethsemane.[4]

It's okay for our communities to be small. The important thing is that we are *in* a community.

Community is a place of vulnerability

"Community," Kara Tippets wrote. "It is the only way to know and be known. It's where we see our own humanity and frailty, our gifts and our weaknesses."[5] Jesus allowed the humanity and frailty He felt to show within His community. During His darkest pre-crucifixion moment in Gethsemane, He tells his three closest friends, "My soul is very sorrowful, even to death; remain here, and watch with me" (Matt. 26:38). He doesn't attempt to mask the turmoil He feels; instead He invites His friends to be there for Him during it.

Researcher-storyteller Brené Brown notes that people in her research "who have a strong sense of love and belonging"[6] are those who are most vulnerable. She explains:

They didn't talk about vulnerability being comfortable, nor did they really talk about it being excruciating. . . . They just talked about it being necessary. They talked about the willingness to say, "I love you" first . . . the willingness to do something where there are no guarantees . . . the willingness to breathe through waiting for the doctor to call after your mammogram. Their willingness to invest in a relationship that may or may not work out. They thought this was fundamental.[7]

True community requires that we are willing, as Jesus was, to be vulnerable with our close friends and family.

PRACTICAL WAYS TO BUILD COMMUNITY

Where can you find your one or two or, if you're like my outgoing girl, your ten or fifteen friends? Here are a few of the basic, fundamental ways you can build community.

Attend a church and get involved

If you aren't actively involved in a local church, you're missing out on one way to build relationships. Church is where you're most likely to meet others who share your values, beliefs, and priorities.

Meet your neighbors

When I say "neighbors," I mean your physical neighbors; those people who live in closest proximity to your house. While it's likely you won't hit it off with everyone on your street—Ted and I haven't always—there's a good chance you will connect with one or two.

Join a group of people with shared interests

A great way to build community is to seek out others who enjoy the same interests and activities as you do. Like me, do you like to read and write? If so, join a local writer's group or book club. If you like to cook, take a culinary class. Be intentional to connect with others who like the same things you do.

Don't overlook your family

When it comes to community, don't be quick to discount or overlook the value of your family. While not everyone comes from a strong family unit, some of us do. Seek out those siblings, parents, and cousins that you connect with the most.

COMMUNITY AT ITS FULLEST

When we understand why we need community and have practical steps on how to build it, we can actively seek out connection with others. We can embrace a life of "me too" that helps ease the burden of our losses and elevate the joy of our gains.

NOTES

Prologue

1. J. R. R. Tolkien, *The Return of the King* (New York: Mariner Books, 1955), 1007.
2. N. D. Wilson, *Death by Living: Life Is Meant to Be Spent* (Nashville, TN: Thomas Nelson, 2013), 5–6.
3. Shauna Niequist, *Bittersweet: Thoughts on Change, Grace, and Learning the Hard Way* (Grand Rapids: Zondervan, 2010), 187.

Control

1. Joni Eareckson Tada and Steven Estes, *When God Weeps: Why Our Sufferings Matter to the Almighty* (Grand Rapids: Zondervan, 1997), 125.

Relationships

1. C. S. Lewis, *The Four Loves* (New York: Harcourt, 1960), 121.
2. *Casablanca: 70th Anniversary*, Blu-ray and book, directed by Michael Curtiz (1942; USA: Warner Bros Entertainment, 2012).
3. Bosley Crowther, "'Casablanca,' With Humphrey Bogart and Ingrid Bergman, at Hollywood—'White Cargo' and 'Ravaged Earth' Open," *The New York Times*, November 27, 1942, http://www.nytimes.com/movie/review?res=9C06E1DF1039E33BBC4F51DFB7678389659EDE.
4. *Dictionary.com*, "interdependence," http://www.dictionary.com/browse/interdependence?s=t.
5. Suzanne Gosselin, "Venting and Losing," *Ungrind*, 2007, http://ungrind.org/2007/venting-and-losing/.
6. C. S. Lewis, *The Magician's Nephew* (New York: HarperCollins, 1999), 154.

Home

1. *Little House on the Prairie,* "Little House on the Prairie," Episode 1, directed by Michael Landon, written by Blanche Hanalis and based on books by Laura Ingalls Wilder. NBC, March 30, 1974.
2. J. R. R. Tolkien, *The Hobbit* (New York: Mariner Books, 2012), 6.
3. Maya Angelou, Twitter post, March 10, 2014, 1:30 p.m., https://twitter.com/DrMayaAngelou/status/443106557836800000?rcf_src=twsrc%5Etfw.
4. *Dictionary.com,* "sojourn," http://www.dictionary.com/browse/sojourn?s=t.

Jobs

1. Jacquelyn Smith, "30 Motivational Quotes for Job Seekers," *Forbes,* January 30, 2014, http://www.forbes.com/sites/jacquelynsmith/2013/01/30/30-motivational-quotes-for-job-seekers/#5ba64971fa8e.
2. Jeff Manion, *The Land Between: Finding God in Difficult Transitions* (Grand Rapids: Zondervan, 2012), 15.
3. Ibid., 17.
4. Genesis 2:15.
5. Google, "confidence," https://www.google.com/search?q=Dictionary#dobs=confidence.
6. Ibid.
7. *Merriam-Webster Online,* "betray," http://www.merriam-webster.com/dictionary/betray.
8. *Thesarus.com,* "betrayal," http://www.thesaurus.com/browse/betrayal?s=t.
9. *Dictionary.com,* "convicted," http://www.dictionary.com/browse/convicted.
10. "Condemnation versus Conviction," *GreatBibleStudy.com,* http://www.greatbiblestudy.com/condemnation_conviction.php.
11. Rob McDowell, *"Fearanoia: Week Four,"* North Metro Church video, 39:57, August 28, 2016, https://vimeo.com/180616683.

Dreams

1. Mark Twain, *Which Was the Dream? And Other Symbolic Writings of the Later Years*, ed. John S. Tuckey (Los Angeles: University of California Press, 1968), 46.
2. Robin Jones Gunn, *Victim of Grace: When God's Goodness Prevails* (Grand Rapids: Zondervan, 2013), Kindle edition, 22.
3. Ernest Hemingway, *Selected Letters 1917–1961*, ed. Carlos Baker (New York: Scribner, 1981), 200.
4. Irving Howe, "Messages from a Divided Man," *The New York Times on the Web,* March 29, 1981, https://www.nytimes.com/books/99/07/04/specials/hemingway-howe.html.

5. Ibid.

6. *Dictionary.com*, "courage," http://www.dictionary.com/browse/courage. Emphasis mine.

7. *We Bought a Zoo*, Blu-ray, directed by Cameron Crowe (2012; USA: 20th Century Fox Home Entertainment, 2015).

8. Beth Moore, *The Patriarchs: Encountering the God of Abraham, Isaac, and Jacob Study Guide* (Nashville, TN: Lifeway Press, 2005), 140.

9. Robin Jones Gunn, *Victim of Grace*, 119.

10. *The Free Dictionary,* "tragedy," http://www.thefreedictionary.com/tragedy.

11. N. D. Wilson, *Death by Living: Life Is Meant to Be Spent* (Nashville, TN: Thomas Nelson, 2013), 71.

12. Ann Voskamp, *One Thousand Gifts Devotional: Reflections on Finding Everyday Graces* (Grand Rapids: Zondervan, 2012), 14.

Health

1. William Samuel Johnson, *Life Hack Quotes*, http://quotes.lifehack.org/quote/william-samuel-johnson/hope-is-necessary-in-every-condition-the/.

2. Joni Eareckson Tada and Steven Estes, *When God Weeps: Why Our Sufferings Matter to the Almighty* (Grand Rapids: Zondervan, 1997), 128.

3. Matthew 9:20–22; Mark 5:25–34; Luke 8:43–48.

4. Liz Curtis Higgs, "The Woman Who Touched Jesus," *Today's Christian Woman*, January 2007, http://www.todayschristianwoman.com/articles/2007/january/woman-who-touched-jesus.html.

5. The International Churchill Society, "Quotes," http://www.winston churchill.org/resources/quotations.

6. Tada and Estes, *When God Weeps,* 129, 130–131.

7. *We Bought a Zoo,* Blu-ray, directed by Cameron Crowe (2012; USA: 20th Century Fox Home Entertainment, 2015).

8. Tada and Estes, *When God Weeps*, 128.

9. *Merriam-Webster Online,* "deus ex machina," https://www.merriam-webster .com/dictionary/deus%20ex%20machina.

10. Kara Tippets and Jill Lynn Buteyn, *Just Show Up* (Colorado Springs, CO: David C. Cook, 2015), 91–92.

Life

1. Lin-Manuel Miranda and Jeremy McCarter, *Hamilton: The Revolution* (New York: Grand Central Publishing, 2016), 91.

2. C. S. Lewis, *A Grief Observed* (San Francisco: HarperOne, 2009), 52.

3. *The Crown*, "Pride & Joy," Season 1, episode 8, directed by Philip Martin, written by Peter Morgan, Netflix, November 4, 2016.

4. Brené Brown, "Boundaries, Empathy, and Compassion," *Path to Opportunity,* March 19, 2016, https://www.youtube.com/watch?v=6NxB6c6d39A &feature=share.

5. Shauna Niequist, *Bittersweet: Thoughts on Change, Grace, and Learning the Hard Way* (Grand Rapids: Zondervan, 2010), 187.

6. American Foundation for Suicide Prevention, "Risk Factors and Warning Signs," https://afsp.org/about-suicide/risk-factors-and-warning-signs/.

7. Helen Keller, *We Bereaved* (New York: Leslie Fulenwider, Inc., 1929), 1.

Epilogue

1. C. S. Lewis, *A Grief Observed* (San Francisco: HarperOne, 2009), 71.

2. Lucy Maud Montgomery, *Anne of Green Gables* (New York: Black and White Classics, 2014), 198. Quote originally by *Pippa Passes.*

Appendix: The Why and How of Community

1. Shauna Niequist, *Bittersweet: Thoughts on Change, Grace, and Learning the Hard Way* (Grand Rapids: Zondervan, 2010), 187.

2. Genesis 2:18.

3. Matthew 17:1–9.

4. Matthew 26:37–38.

5. Kara Tippets and Jill Lynn Buteyn, *Just Show Up* (Colorado Springs, CO: David C. Cook, 2015), 11.

6. Brené Brown, "The Power of Vulnerability," TED Talk, December 2010, https://www.ted.com/talks/brene_brown_on_vulnerability/transcript? language=en.

7. Ibid.

ACKNOWLEDGMENTS

Ted, it's been quite the year. We've moved. We've grieved your dad's death. We've even experienced #theglamoroustourlife. There were weeks when I'd call you on the road, discouragement and defeat in my voice, and cry, "I don't know if I can finish this book." It turns out that writing on loss was more difficult than I ever anticipated, especially in the midst of it. You, in your distinctly Ted-way, would tell me to just keep writing. And somehow, I would. I'm grateful that in better and in worse, in sickness and in health, in good times and in bad, that we're in it together. You and me, always and forever, "Team Us."

Olivia, Ava, Savannah, and Dorothy: thank you for allowing me to share some of your stories in this book, too. Your tender hearts and generous spirits daily inspire me. It's such an honor to watch you grow. I love you!

Mom and Dad, you were the first two people to love me, to encourage me, and to read my writing. Decades later, you still faithfully cheer me on. This book absolutely would not exist if it weren't for you both. Sarah, Hayley, and Kaitlyn, I always proudly tell people that I have three sisters. Thank you for your continued love, support, and laughter over the years. Jake, I'm so glad you are now officially a part of the family.

Alice, I will always remember how excited, supportive, and proud Ed was when *Team Us* was published. Both you and Ed lovingly welcomed me into your family fifteen years ago and I'm better because of it. Ruth and Jim, I'm so very grateful for all the ways you've loved and encouraged me since I married Ted. Pam, when I think of this book, I fondly recall our back-porch, rocking-chair conversation in Wisconsin when we were both there for Ed's funeral. I was in the early stages of writing and I was already weary. You listened and encouraged me, and I'm grateful.

To the team at Moody—John, Zack, Ashley, and Randall—thank you for all your hard work on and investment in this project. I deeply appreciate each of you and the excitement and excellence you have brought to the process. Linda Joy and Connor, thank you for your editorial expertise and all the ways your thoughts and suggestions have made this book stronger. I firmly believe that an editor makes a book better and you are both evidence of that!

Thank you to the friends who bravely shared with me their own stories of personal loss. Denise, Rhonda, Carlie, Megan, Salina, Rebecca, Julie, and Keri, as well as those friends who wished to remain anonymous, you are my heroes. I am truly honored and humbled that you would trust me with your experiences. Your words and your faith have moved me deeply.

I'm also grateful to the friends and family who read chapters, gave me feedback, and encouraged and prayed for me along the way. These include, but are certainly not limited to: Liz, Rhonda, Julie, Shona, Megan, Samantha, and my mom.

To Jenny Schroedel—what a joy it was to interview you on grief. Your book *Naming the Child* was such a comfort to me following my miscarriage.

North Metro pastors, staff, and family members, thank you for always making church feel like home.

Finally, thank You, Lord. In the writing of this book, You have pushed me to grow and stretch in new and uncomfortable ways. There have been many moments when I've resisted and questioned. Through it all, though, I've been continually reminded that You, the Author of my story, are right beside me.

What many marriages
are missing...

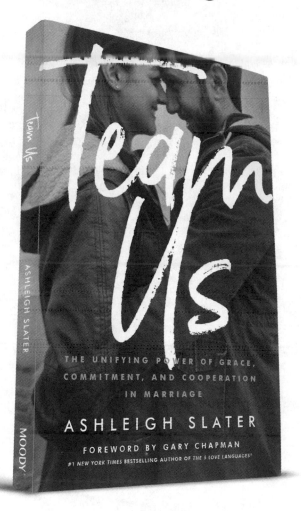

Scripture's cure
for the worry epidemic

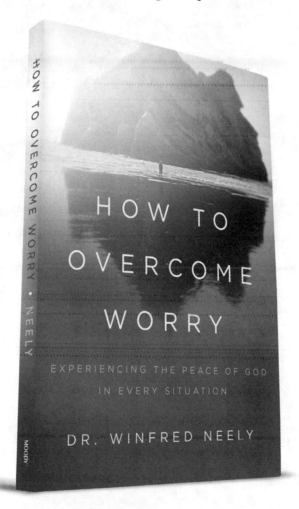

DISCARD